SUPERNATURAL
ABUNDANCE
A JOURNEY TO THE FATHER'S HOUSE

LEIF HETLAND

Dedication

I want to dedicate this book to my daughter, Courtney Rebekka Hetland. I know that she is living out the Father's supernatural abundance in her life. I am so proud of the young woman she is becoming and know she will go far in life!

Love you Courtney Bek!
Dad

Table of Contents

A Message from Leif

What follows is a story derived from a vision that the Holy Spirit gave me a few years ago. I was asking him how to help others access the amazing abundance that is available in God's Kingdom. Learning to seize the bounty of heaven is not a skill to be developed, but the result of a transformed heart and a renewed mind. Rather than try and simply teach the ways of *supernatural abundance*, I decided to start with a story. Maybe not every message in this story will speak to your mind, but I guarantee it will enter your heart. Since I believe that accessing heaven's abundance requires both a mind and heart transformation, I've also included a series of appendices. Some have great quotes to help condition your thought patterns, and the rest are a series of biblical outlines of God's plan for abundance in your life.

Please continue pursuing *supernatural abundance*, using these tools, as well as the ones the Holy Spirit gives you. Too much of God's goodness has remained unclaimed by His children. Let's learn to grab it and steward it together.

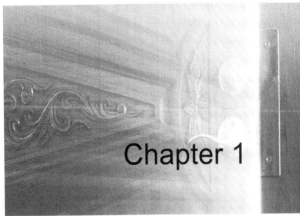

Chapter 1

It was Tuesday. Adam slumped through the door, barely noticing the state of his unkempt apartment. He tossed his keys toward the pile of unopened bills on the couch, dropped into his chair, while not bothering to turn on a light. The TV remote was laid where he left it, and the TV had been on the same channel for hours.

He sat and watched, switching channels whenever a commercial appeared. He fought to block out the thoughts that had been running through his head all day, or, at the very least, drown them out with the sounds coming from the television.

His mind haunted him, *How long has it been like this? How long have I been struggling to keep the shop above water? How long has it been sinking? How long have I been behind on the lease for the shop? How long has it been since I've paid rent on the apartment? How long before they shut off my lights?*

Beads of sweat formed on his forehead, and a sick feeling began to boil deep in his stomach. He changed the channel and turned up the volume, cramming every worry into a dark pile in the corner of his mind.

Adam was well into his third rerun of an old sitcom when the phone rang. The shock of a sound coming from anywhere but the glowing box on the far side of the room caused him to jump to his feet with alarm. His eyes darted from left to right, searching for the source of the sound. The sound blasting from the television made it difficult, so he walked over and mashed the off button. He quickly found the phone under a crumpled pile of food wrappers near his chair, and fumbled his thumb to the answer button.

"Hello," he said taking in a deep breath.

"Hello son."

Adam felt his hands go numb. It had been years since he had heard that voice, but it was as immediately familiar as the feeling of the ground under his feet.

"Dad," The word felt dry in his mouth, making the

rest of his sentence get caught somewhere in the back of his throat. Adam had ignored so many calls – thrown away so many unopened letters. What do you say after you've worked so hard to say nothing?

"I know that it's been a long time," his Father said, filling the gap in the conversation, "but I still want to talk to you."

Adam remained silent.

"Now, I know you don't want to talk to me and that's alright."

Adam bit his lip. Holding back tears or a shout, he couldn't tell which.

"I have a gift I want to give you. What you do with it is entirely up to you." Despite the palpable tension, Adam's Father maintained a gentle tone, "You can keep and care for it, or you can leave it alone. All I ask is that you come see it."

His Father paused, waiting for a response. When He didn't get one, He asked, "Did you get the letter I sent you?"

Adam looked back at the small mountain of mail on

his couch and answered, "Yes."

"Good, then I hope to be seeing you soon. I love you, son."

Those last four words landed like four hot pokers in Adam's ear, causing him to cringe and blurt out, "You know I don't need anything. I don't need any help."

"I know, son."

Silence.

Adam's Father took in a long breath and said, "I hope to see you soon."

After the line went silent, Adam dropped the phone back into the pile of wrappers and slumped onto the couch next to the pile of mail. He absently pushed through the pile with one hand, causing a small avalanche of bills to fall to the floor. It was easy to find his Father's letter, it was the only one written by hand.

Adam,

You are my son. It has been too long since we have spoken. Just this morning I was walking through the vineyards where we used to spend so much time together. We played so many games of hide and seek. I suppose it's no different now. You always were the best at hiding. Now it's time for me to hide for you, though I'm sure you know where to find me.

It's time to come home. I have something to give you.

I Love you,
Your Dad

His Father's signature adorned the bottom of the page. Adam had seen that signature on every check his Father had sent before he tore it up.

"Why?" he asked the empty room, "Why now?"

Adam noticed an airplane ticket hanging partway out of the opened envelope. The flight left early the next morning. A deep ache formed in the pit of his stomach. Though the thought of having to face all of the pain that had been shared between him and his Father was overwhelming, the thought of staying here to wait for the bill collectors to come knocking was even more overwhelming.

The brief contents of the letter and phone call were the most Adam had heard his Father say in over five years. Part of him wanted to hang on to his anger and disappointment, but the other part was so inexplicably relieved that it made him light headed. Maybe it was just that he was at the end of his rope, or maybe enough time had finally passed. He wasn't sure. Mixed as his emotions were, clarity had come to Adam's mind that had been gone for far too long. He may not be sure why, but he had to go.

Adam fought to keep his nerves under control. He tried to read a magazine article on the flight, but gave up after he reread the first paragraph for the third time, unable to retain any of its contents. Was he excited? Scared? Yes. Last night had been the first time he had heard his Father's voice in years. The idea of seeing Him face to face made his hands shake.

After his plane landed, Adam rushed through the crowded airport, his small suitcase knocking into knees and rolling over toes behind him. He was looking for a taxi to flag down when he heard a voice.

"Hello Adam."

Adam turned to see a gray-haired man with neatly combed hair and piercing grey-blue eyes, "Howard?"

"Happy to hear that the years have not made me completely unrecognizable," the man smiled, "I am here to take you to your Father's house."

Howard Smith had been the keeper and caretaker of his Father's estate for longer than Adam could remember. Wherever there was a torn shirt or scraped knee, Howard was there. Whenever a baseball went through a window or a faucet spouted muddy water, he was there and moments later the problem was solved.

"You haven't aged a day." Adam said with a grin.

"I can't say the same for you. You were a skinny mess of unkempt hair and unbridled energy last time I saw you. A man has grown around the boy I knew." Howard replied.

Adam gave a sheepish smile.

"Come." Howard said, laughing as he gestured toward a black limousine parked nearby. "Your Father is waiting."

Ducking into the backseat of the limo, Adam began to feel the tingling nervousness rise in his stomach again. His Father was a wealthy man who regularly used His wealth for the benefit of others. He had always admired this, but whenever this generosity was pointed at him, Adam felt uneasy. Humility was what he called it in his mind. Many people took advantage of his Father's quickness to give. Adam never wanted to be one of them.

Alone in the back of the limousine, there was nothing to distract from the anxious excitement growing in Adam's chest. What was his Father going to say? What was this gift? All these questions washed from his mind as his childhood home appeared from over the horizon.

Built on a cliff overlooking the ocean, his Father's house was an architectural masterpiece. Acres of lush farmland overflowing with every kind of fruit and vegetable filled the landscape with color. The rising sun glinted off the many tall windows that overlooked the countryside. Though the estate was adorned with many tall stone pillars, intricate brass fixtures, and thick stonewalls, it always felt like a home. Even visitors that were not accustomed to such extravagance would often remark about the comfort of the estate.

The limousine drove up the cobblestone path and came to stop near the large front door, which his

Father had carved by hand. Adam remembered seeing it come together piece by piece in his Father's shop. How long ago had that been?

Howard jumped out of the driver seat and opened the door for Adam.

"You don't have to do that, Howard," said Adam.

"And you didn't have to come," he answered, "but here we are."

Adam smiled and stepped out of the car. The salty sea air, mixed with the sweet aroma of the nearby flower gardens, brought back more memories than he could count. Adam had been gone for so long that he had forgotten how much he had left behind.

Howard shut the car door and reached behind his back, "These are for you." He produced a large ring of keys.

"And Father?" He asked, giving the keys a cursory look.

"Waiting for you inside," Howard answered. "Go on. I'll be just behind."

Adam reached out and took the keys. The ring was large enough to fit around an apple. It held over a dozen keys of every size and shape. All of the keys were unfamiliar to Adam, all except one … an old-fashioned brass key in the shape of an eagle.

When his Father built His house, the last thing He finished was the front door. After it was done, He had a special key made for each of His children. Each one was different, but they all opened the front door to His house. Adam's key had been made in the shape of an eagle. The last time he had seen it was the day he threw it into the ocean; the day he left his Father's house for good.

His heart racing, Adam took his key in hand and approached the door. There he paused a moment. He could still leave. Howard would drive him back to the airport. He wouldn't be happy about it, but he would do it. Then he wouldn't have to face his Father and all that was between them. There was still a choice. Feeling the anxiety and excitement battle within his chest, he slid the key into the lock and turned it with a deep echoing click.

Chapter 2

The door swung open on well-oiled hinges. Adam stepped into the immaculate entryway. The room had seemed immense when he was a child; an endless cavern lined with hand carved mahogany molding and brass fixed lamps. It was not so different now. Streams of sunlight flowed down from the domed skylight, painting patterns on the hardwood floor. Even though Adam was significantly taller and older now, it was hard to resist the feeling of warmth that the room created. Everything held a hundred memories – the tall coat racks that were full during winter, as well as the shoe shelves that had held so many muddy boots and dirty sneakers. Even the echoing sound his feet made on the hardwood was as familiar as the sound of his own breath.

He turned, taking it all in, and then smacked his hand over his eyes as he saw the portrait that hung on the wall just to the right of the front door.

Why does he have to do that? Adam muttered to himself, looking at the portrait through his fingers.

Adam's Father had many children. An artist had been commissioned to paint portraits of each of them. Of course, Father had insisted that each one be done on the largest available canvas. This resulted in there not being nearly enough walls in the house to hold all of the massive portraits. Realizing this, Adam's Father had decided that He would display one of His children's portraits in the entryway. A different portrait would be displayed every day so that everyone had a chance to be shown. This way his Father would always communicate to each of his children that they were the most important person in his house.

The portrait that hung in the entryway featured a thin-faced, freckled boy, with dark brown hair and a mischievous smile.

"It has been a long time since I've seen that smile." Howard remarked.

Adam turned, "What's he up to, Howard?"

"I'm sorry?" Howard replied.

"Why is he toying with me?" Adam looked back at the portrait of his younger self.

Howard placed a hand on Adam's shoulder, letting it rest there a moment before saying, "He's not toying with you."

Adam pulled away and threw the ring of keys on the ground, "Then why the games, the notes, the keys, and this old painting? What's the point?"

The old caretaker sighed and picked up the keys, "I know that you and your Father did not leave each other happily. There is a deep pain separating the two of you. I know your Father has His own way of going about things, but I also know that all He wants is for things to be made right between the two of you."

Adam took in a few deep breaths, trying not to feel embarrassed by his outburst.

"And something tells me that you want things to be made right as well." contorted Adam. Howard smiled, "Let Him say the things He's been waiting to say. And let Him say it in His way. He always has reason for it."

Adam pinched the bridge of His nose and then rubbed his eyes. He had come this far; turning back now would be such a waste. And something deep in his heart was still desperate to see his Father again.

"Alright, Howard. I'll see what He has to say."

"I thought you might," said Howard, reaching into his coat pocket and producing a small yellow envelope. "I was told to give you this when you were ready to find your Father."

Adam reached out and took it, recognizing his own name written on the front in his Father's handwriting. Inside was a small note, also written by hand:

Son,

Thank you so much for deciding to come. It's been my great desire to see you face to face again. There has been much that has gone unsaid between us, too much. I hope you will indulge me a little further. There is so much that I want to say to you, but some things are better shown than told. So come find me. Howard will help you, just as he always has. Start where things always started. I'll see you soon.

Once again, that all too familiar signature sat at the

bottom of the page.

"Well, Howard," Adam laughed, "in for a penny, in for a pound. Let's see what the old man has cooked up."

"Indeed." said Howard, holding back a chuckle.

The massive entryway led into a long and well-lit hall, lined by dozens of dark wooden doors. Each led to one of the many rooms that made up his Father's mansion. Much of Adam's childhood had been spent running up and down these halls, chasing one of his siblings or even his Father. Adam had forgotten how much time his Father had spent playing with him. He was different from most other Father's in that respect. There was always more than enough business to take care of, but He was always quick to make time for His children.

Adam's eyes were drawn to the first door on the left, a tall piece of oak with the words carved neatly above it: 'You're Attitude Determines Your Outlook'.

"The Study." Howard said, looking at the door.

"Oh, I remember. Every lesson, every lecture, every time a window was broken or the fine china used as hockey pucks." Adam answered. He laughed at the memory, "Every important conversation started here in his study."

Adam tried the doorknob, but found it locked. He frowned for a moment, but then remembered the keys. He turned to find Howard holding the ring out in front of him.

"Still picking up after you," said the old caretaker.

Adam smiled, taking the keys, "I'll learn one day."

He then found a small silver key with the word 'Attitude' embossed across it.

"What is it Father used to say?" Adam asked sliding the silver key into the lock, "The right attitude can unlock any door!'"

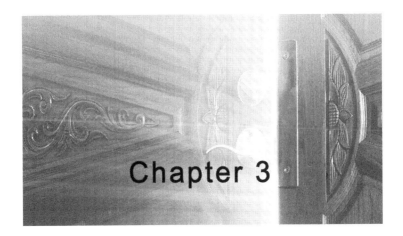

Chapter 3

The study was a quiet place. There were no visible walls, only shelves filled to the brim with books of every size, shape, and age. The sunlight poured in through ceiling-high windows, bringing even more warmth out of the antique chairs and his Father's thick oak desk. It was a place of learning and teaching, of speaking and listening.

Adam stepped into the room, feeling the familiar creak of floorboards beneath his feet. He spotted his Father's old globe, a massive marble ball, mounted in a polished brass frame. He gave it a spin as he walked past. A large leather bound ledger sat closed on the center of the desk. Across the cover the words 'Adam's Tire Repair and Replace' were embossed in gold lettering.

"He's been keeping an eye on my business?" Adam

asked, turning toward Howard.

The caretaker shrugged, "Your Father keeps an eye on everything."

"Just as well, there isn't much to see anyway," Adam said, sinking into the chair in front of the desk. "Just a mediocre start followed by a slow and steady decline."

"Your Father told me about the grand opening. It didn't sound mediocre."

Adam traced the letters on the ledger with the tip of his finger, "He did come to that, didn't He?"

Howard settled into the chair on the opposite side of the desk, "It was–"

"It was the last time I saw Him," Adam interrupted. "We didn't even speak. I didn't speak, I should say."

The memory was still fresh in Adam's mind. He had tied balloons and colored banners all throughout the shop. He was no interior decorator. They had been messy and tied with big ugly knots, but he was elated all the same. This was the culmination of all his hard work. His first business – the first thing he had truly done on his own. Only about a dozen people had shown up, but it felt like a thousand to him. He had even given a short speech while standing on a small stack of tires.

He noticed his Father just as he was finishing up his speech. He was standing at the back of the crowd, applauding as Adam stepped down from his rubber stage. Adam tried to pretend like he hadn't seen Him, but it was also hard not to stare. Why had his Father come? Was it to patronize him, or to see if Adam could handle things himself? Eventually Adam found himself glaring at his Father from across the room. Finally, after what seemed like hours, his Father closed the gap.

He rested His hand on Adam's shoulder, but Adam shrugged it off.

"That's alright, son," his Father said, looking at the rejected hand. "I just wanted to come to congratulate you."

Adam tried to give an obligatory smile, but the attempt made him sick to his stomach. Without a word, he turned and marched straight to his newly built office, slamming the door behind him. He stayed there, fuming, until closing time.

"He waited until your employees told Him they had to close." Howard said.

Adam snapped out of the memory, "What?"

"I drove him to your shop that day," Howard adjusted his position in the chair. "He waited for you to come back out until they had to lock down the building."

"I felt so justified in my anger that day." Adam went back to tracing the letters on the ledger, "It's different looking back."

"Yes?"

"Some of this is my fault too, I guess," Adam said looking up at the old caretaker. "I've thrown away a lot of chances to make things right."

Howard reached across the desk and flipped open the ledger. Inside was a detailed record of every penny that came in and out of Adam's tire company. Every loan payment, every month's rent, every tire, every repair, every pack of chips sold from the vending machine ... all of it. Adam flipped through the pages, just as he had so many times with his own records. In the middle of the book he found a graph outlining the profits and losses his company had undergone throughout the years. Though there were many ups and downs, his business showed a clear and steady downward trend.

Adam had known this, of course. Lately, he had spent most of his days worrying about it. But what he hadn't known was that his Father had been keeping notes the entire time. At each place where the graph dipped close to, or sometimes well below the red line, his Father had jotted down a little note.

I should give Adam a call. I'll send him a letter. Maybe I'll speak with the bank. I'll try and visit again. Each was different, but every dip in Adam's finances was paired with at least one of the small handwritten notes. Adam thought back for a moment. He had thrown away dozens of letters, stopped answering the phone entirely, and slammed the door in his Father's face on more than one occasion, but he had never realized the timing of these regular visits and messages.

Maybe it was because so much of his time had been spent fretting over the fate of the business, or maybe it was because of all the anger he felt toward his Father. But Adam had never seen these attempted calls and visits as a helping hand. Taking advice would mean that he couldn't figure it out himself.

Calling in favors would be like cheating at a game of cards, and cashing the checks his Father sent would have felt like signing a contract that said, "You couldn't do it on your own, Adam."

A small spot of water appeared on the ledger, blurring some of the ink on one of his Father's notes. Then another drop appeared, and another. Adam realized that tears were dripping from the tip of his nose.

"I wanted to show Him that I could do it myself," Adam said, wiping his face. "I grew up around the signs of my Father's success. Everything He did was great. I wanted to show Him that I could do it on my own."

"Oh Adam!" Howard leaned forward and looked him strait in the eyes, "You can't show him what He's already seen."

He gave a small involuntary headshake, "What?"

"Do you remember the last time you and your Father were in this room together?"

Adam thought. He must have been in his late teens. It was a sunny day like this one. He knew this because he remembered feeling the warmth of the sun coming through the tall windows. His Father was sitting at the desk, while Adam stood at His side, looking over His shoulder. Together they were going over the ledger for his Father's fields and cattle. They were discussing the amount of feed that would be needed for the month, and how best to distribute the labor between his Father's many workers. It was a simple memory. Adam remembered nothing particularly special about that day, though it was one of the last happy moments that he and his Father had spent together.

"We were going over the ledger for the farm," Adam said, looking at the old caretaker. "Just business as usual."

"Indeed," Howard said with a smile. "And why, may I ask, do you think your Father would invite you in on His 'business as usual?'"

This made Adam pause. His Father had always talked about how He went about His business. He enjoyed input, advice, and opinions. Wasn't that normal?

Howard continued before Adam could answer, "You were assigning all the shifts for the fields by the time you were sixteen. Your Father had you setting the prices for half His exports by seventeen. Just a few more years and you would have been running His entire farm."

Adam still remained silent.

"You didn't have to show Him that you could do anything on your own because He already knew." The old caretaker took in a deep breath, "He trusts you, Adam. He always has."

Adam could feel tears beginning to form at the corners of his eyes again. He looked back at the ledger on the desk in front of him. So many little notes. So many moments when his Father wanted to come and help him get back on his feet. He had forgotten how much he had been put in charge of when he was young. His Father would pop in from time to time, making suggestions and asking questions. At the time, it hadn't occurred to Adam that his Father probably knew how to run the farm much better than he did. His Father had shown so much restraint, letting Adam make mistakes and find solutions. Always guiding, while allowing Adam to lead. That was how it had always been.

"I suppose I should have returned His trust, right Howard?"

The old caretaker tilted his head.

Adam stood up and took a few steps toward the windows, "He never took over after He put me in charge of the fields. He let me run them the way I wanted. Why didn't I trust Him to let me find success on my own?"

Howard stood up and laughed, "You read the words every time you enter this room. It's why your Father wrote them over the door."

Adam remembered the mantra etched over the entrance to the study Your Attitude Determines Your Outlook.

"Your Father is nothing if not a teacher." Howard continued, "He teaches with everything He does … the writing over the door, embossing the word attitude on the key to this room. It all conveys the same message: You can see this world and the people in it many different ways, but you will never see them properly unless you have the right attitude."

Adam looked back at the ledger, remembering all the times his Father had told him the same thing. Seeing the complete record of his struggles, it made a lot more sense than it did when he was young.

"Alright," Adam said. "Where is He?"

"Where is who?" Howard asked.

"Where is my Father?" Adam closed the ledger asking, "I've seen what He has to say, now where is He?

"Oh Adam, we've only just started. He has much more to tell you." The caretaker laughed and held out another sealed envelope.

*S*on, I always have and always will love you. The pain between us has made it hard for me to show my love to you. I want you to be your own man, but I don't want you to give up the connection between us. Now I want to show you some of what's been lost. Go to the place where old things are made new. I will see you soon.

Adam knew where his Father wanted him to go as soon as he finished the note. He led the way out of the study, down the hall, and out the back door.

The back porch was Adam's favorite place in is Father's house. It was a massive redwood deck that was built right up to the edge of the cliff that overlooked both the ocean and the fields. The endless glistening waves were paralleled by the equally endless rows of orange trees, wheat fields, and vineyards that made up his Father's fields. Together these perfect patches of Earth and ocean stretched to the horizon. Adam had never been anywhere more beautiful.

The cool air coming in from the sea was mixed with the warmth that came from the valley. His Father used to say that one could smell all the good things in the world from that spot. It felt true every time Adam stood there, even though the place now held as many painful memories as good. He lingered there for only a moment, and then turned and started down the path that ran along the cliff.

Adam and the old caretaker made their way around the side of the house until they came upon a small wooden building. His Father called it a shed, but in truth it was much more than that. Most of the fixtures, carvings, and statuary that adorned his Father's house came from that shed, each crafted by his Father's hand. This was also the place Adam would go whenever anything of his was broken. If his bike got a flat tire, when a toy soldier got snapped in two, or roughhousing resulted in a chair being torn to pieces, it all got put back together in that shed.

"You know how your Father thinks."

Adam turned back and looked at Howard.

"You haven't hesitated for a moment after you read His clues. You know exactly where He wants you to go."

Adam smiled, "Or maybe He knows how I think."

The shed was a building in the simplest sense. It had four walls, a lean-to roof, and a plain wooden door. Adam had once asked why his Father hadn't built a more substantial workshop, especially since he liked to build things so much. His Father had said, "I like having beautiful things come from an ordinary place. It makes them more beautiful."

Adam tried the door, but found it locked. Not surprised, he pulled the ring of keys from his coat pocket. He knew which key would open the door, but couldn't find it. Immediately, Howard reached into his coat pocket.

"Ah yes," the old caretaker said. "I nearly forgot. Your Father asked that I not give you this key until we arrive at the shed." He pulled out a rough hewn iron key, "Thought it might give a little too much of the surprise away."

Adam knew the key well. As soon as each child was old enough to use a hammer, Father would take them to the shed to make a key. He helped each one heat the iron and held it steady as they hammered. After the child thought the key was right, Father would dip the key in cold water and try it on the lock. If it didn't work, He would then reheat it and they would try again. Sometimes it only took a few attempts, and sometimes it took dozens.

Once the key finally worked, Father would give it to the child and say, '*Now you may come to the shed any time you'd like. You can build, and you can create. And now that you know it may take a few tries before your creations work, you also know that, with enough practice, you can make anything work.*'

Adam rubbed his finger over the small letter "A" that he had etched in his key so many years ago. It had taken him thirty-nine tries to get the key to work right. Father had stayed with him into the night, patiently heating and reheating the key. Offering encouragement and advice as it was needed.

Adam stuck his key in the lock. It took a little fiddling, but it turned and the door swung open.

The shed looked different than Adam remembered. It

used to be filled with every kind of tool and building material imaginable. It used to smell like fresh cut wood and steam. Now it smelled like dust. In place of the tools and workbenches that normally adorned the walls, there were only rusted bicycles, discolored sporting equipment, and dried buckets of paint. Everything was covered in cobwebs and dust.

"Howard, why is everything so..." Adam was struck silent as his eye caught something in the middle of the pile of junk.

A portrait sat lopsided on a pile of worn out baseball gloves. It was the same size and style as the portraits that his Father used to hang in His entryway. This one depicted a girl, freckle faced with long brown hair, and a smile that was infectious even under a layer of dust.

"Susanna," Adam said with that familiar dryness filling his mouth.

Susanna Greene came into Adam's life when he was still young. She didn't live far from his Father's house. One summer she chased a rabbit all the way from her backyard to the front field near Father's house, hoping to make it a pet. Adam was in the middle of a game of hide and seek with his brother when Susanna ran into him at full speed. Once the two realized what had happened, they spent the rest of the day chasing the rabbit together. They never did catch it, but they became best friends instantly. Susanna came over almost every day after that. Father took a liking to her straight away, saying that He'd adopt her into the family. This, of course, is something He'd say when just about anyone visited His home. He'd had the portrait made of her shortly after that.

"You were inseparable," Howard said, a big grin stretched across his face.

"I thought so too," Adam said, thumbing through the keys, "But it didn't turn out that way."

Howard gripped him on the shoulder, "I know it was hard."

"Hard?" Adam said, stepping away. "She left me just as my business was falling apart. She left me alone while I was losing everything." He let out a few hot breaths, "It wasn't hard. It was crushing!"

Howard's face remained the perfect picture of peace and patience. He waited a moment and then asked, "And why did she leave?"

Adam felt anger try to leap out of his chest, but instead he let out a cold sigh, "We hardly spoke near the end. I was pushing so hard. Everything was going into the business, everything I had."

"I was going to propose," he rubbed the tears away before they could form. "Just as soon as things started looking better, I was going to do it. Just as soon as I could afford a ring that was good enough."

The old caretaker waited to make sure that Adam was done speaking, then he said, "Look around." He pointed at the old piles, "What is all this?"

There was so much that Adam had a hard time focusing on any one thing. On the far side of the room he saw an old kite he had built when he was thirteen. The fabric had several holes and some of the wood was broken. The racecar he built with his brothers when he was ten was on top of one of the piles. The potato gun he made when he was nine, the cards he collected when he was fifteen, the baseball bat he carved when he was eleven; this was everything he used to play with and everything he had ever made.

"When you were young your life was led by passion," Howard said. "You created things because you were excited about them. You worked. Oh, you worked hard. You spent weeks on that racecar. You spent hours organizing those baseball cards, and you made countless toys and trinkets for Susanna."

Adam looked back at the portrait as Howard continued, "But something got lost along the way. You started working to prove something, and then you started working to stay afloat. You are a creator, Adam, just like your Father. You are meant to create out of passion. Don't get me wrong, there's nothing wrong with starting a tire shop. Your Father was just as passionate about building a doorframe as He was about sculpting one of His statues. But you didn't start your business out of passion; you started it out of pain. And then you fought to keep it afloat out of fear."

A feeling was welling up in Adam's chest again. It was that feeling that kept him from speaking to his Father for all these years. Pride, anger, fear ... he didn't know what to call it. But for the first time he knew he had to let it go. He had to choose to let it go!

Howard smiled, "I know there has been pain between you and your Father. But look at all you've given up by holding on to that pain."

Even coming back to the house had shown that, Adam thought. It had been a long time since he had felt anything as good as the comfort and warmth of his Father's house. Susanna had been the last bastion of light in his world, his last beacon of hope. When she left he felt lost and abandoned. He had assumed that she left because of how hard everything had become. But now he wondered if it was him that she was running from.

"Ok Howard," Adam sighed, resting his hand on the caretaker's shoulder. "How do I get it all back?"

Without a word Howard reached into his coat pocket and pulled out another letter. Adam took it and saw his name written on the front just like the others. This time, however, it was not is Father's handwriting. The tight looping letters looked just the same as they had on so many passed notes during school. It was Susanna's.

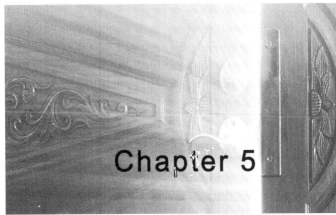

Chapter 5

*A*dam, I miss you. Not just because we haven't seen each other. I miss the Adam that I grew up with. I don't know when that Adam got lost, but he did. Now you are on your way to finding him again and I couldn't be happier. I'm sorry that I left, but I couldn't stand by and watch you work the man I love to death. I wish I'd known how to help you then, but I didn't. Thankfully your Father knows just what to do. So keep going, Adam. And come find me when you've found yourself again. It's what I've been waiting for. You should start looking in the place where your dreams came from.

I'll see you soon,
Susanna

Adam folded the note and put it in his pocket, biting

his lip to hold back the tears. He had been so overwhelmed by the slow and steady collapse of his business that he had been numb when Susanna left. It had been hard enough to keep his head above water as it was, thinking about her would have pulled him straight to the bottom of the ocean. So every day he worked, and every night he filled his mind with every distraction available. It would have been too painful to do anything else.

"She came here to visit your Father just after," Howard said, interrupting Adams thoughts.

"After what?" Adam asked, not looking at the old caretaker.

"Well, after she left you."

Adam didn't respond.

"They talked for hours," Howard said, looking out a nearby window. "I did my best not to eavesdrop on their conversation, but I heard enough to know that she didn't leave because she wanted to get away from you. She left so that she could find out how to get closer to you."

Adam scoffed, "You think I'm lying?"

"No, but…"

"She loves you, Adam," Howard interrupted. "She always has, and I'm quite certain that she always will. But for some reason you believed that you had to prove yourself to her, just as you believe that you have to prove yourself to your Father."

Adam finally turned to face Howard, and for the first time in all his memory, he saw tears in the old caretaker's eyes.

"I don't know why you think you have to prove so much to so many, but you're wrong!" The tears were flowing freely now, "And in deciding that you have to prove yourself, that you have to prove your worth, you have built a great stone wall between you and everyone that loves you."

"Howard," Adam rested a hand on his shoulder.

Howard continued, "I understand why you sit alone night after night. I understand why you've gone in to work everyday feeling number than the last. You've carried a mountain of expectation on your back for so long. Everything you are has been riding on something that is falling apart." The old caretaker wiped the tears from his face, straightened up, and looked directly into Adam's eyes, "What I don't understand is why you would leave your identity tied to a ship that is sinking, especially when everyone who loves you keep throwing out lifelines?"

Something shifted deep in Adam's stomach. After he and his Father had their falling out, Adam had been so determined to show that he was capable. He started the tire business because it was the first opportunity that presented itself. The necessary partnerships fell easily into place, and Adam's own natural talent for business and strategy made everything come together quickly and efficiently. He had been proud of how well things had been put together, and rightly so. He had done it all himself. When everything started to come apart, when customers stopped showing up, when bills started piling up; he started to panic. The proof of his success, his value, was coming apart at the seams. Adam had fought like a cornered rat, because he felt like a cornered rat.

"Your Father would have helped you," said Howard. "He would have given you a loan. He would have given you cash outright if you would have let him. He would have brought in advertisers, business consultants, partnerships; He would have brought you anything. And then, if everything still failed, even if the business still fell apart, He would have funded your next idea. Why? Because He believes in you!"

The weight in Adam's stomach did another sharp turn. He wanted the business to be a success so badly. It was all he had thought about for years. He had poured everything he had into that company. His time, his money, his relationships, he had sacrificed them all. But why? If it was failing, why not just try something new? Why not start over?

Then the warm dawn of understanding rose in Adam's mind. He wasn't fighting to save the business. He was fighting to save himself. All of his self worth was tied up in that tire shop. If it failed, then he had failed! It was his idea, his work, and his company.

"But I failed!" Adam said under his breath, "The shop is done. It didn't work. I couldn't make it work."

"Oh Adam," Howard smiled, "Why does that matter? How many times did you fail when you tried to make the key to this door? How many times did you fall when you were learning to ride a bike? I've bandaged more of your scrapes and cuts than I care to count. Do you remember what you were doing when I was patching you up?"

"No," He said, looking at the ground.

"You were squirming all over the place, eager to get up and back to whatever had caused the wounding. Failure didn't matter then, and it doesn't matter now. Life is full of success, and falling down is part of it."

Adam scratched the back of his head.

"I'm not your Father," Howard said, "But I have known you just as long as He has. You are not my son, but I don't know how I could love you more. So please hear me when I tell you that your company is not you. It came from you, so it is sad that it has failed. But it is nothing so final as 'failure' for you. It is a small stumble in a long journey. And it is such a tragedy that you would let this small stumble be your journey's end because of a pain between you and your Father."

Adam reached out and embraced the old caretaker. Howard had been such a constant in his life that it was easy to take him for granted. His counsel, his patience, his kindness, and his help, all of it was always there in seemingly limitless supply. Adam hadn't realized that when he left his Father's house, he had left Howard too.

"Thank you," Adam said, feeling the words with every ounce of gratitude he could.

"You don't need to thank me," Howard said, returning the embrace. "Just be the man you always have been. Take down those walls that block the ones who love you. Let us be part of your success story."

"I will," Adam said, feeling Susanna's note in his pocket. "Do you think I can really win her back?"

Howard pulled back so he could again look him in the eye, "I think she wants nothing more than for you to win her back." "I guess there's only one way to find out." Adam took the note out of his pocket and looked at it again.

"Do you know where we are going?" Howard asked.

"Oh yes," Adam answered, "The place where my dreams came from, that would have to be my old bedroom."

Adam loved his room. His Father built and designed a unique room for each of His children. Some of Adam's brothers and sisters had piles of toys so thick that you couldn't see the ground. Others held art supplies and canvases just in case inspiration struck, while some were decorated with posters of famous people or places. But Adam's room was different. In his room he had a bed, a window, and a small brown writing desk. A notebook and one pen on the desk was all the decoration it held. His walls were plain, his floor was empty, and his bed was simple and neat.

Adam was disappointed the first time his Father showed him the room he had made. "You are a dreamer," his Father had said seeing the dissatisfaction, "and this is the room of a dreamer. You have ideas, a great many of them; some will spend all day following you around. When you go to sleep at night, those ideas will leap into your mind and fill your dreams. They will still be fresh in your mind when you wake. Your room is simple and blank so that nothing will distract from the beauty and wonder that will come from your mind. Write down every dream. I want to see them all, and I'm sure the world will too."

And it was true. Ideas came into Adam's mind almost every night. By the time he was ten, he had filled over a dozen notebooks with everything that had come to him in the night. As the years went by he came to love the simple serenity that he felt in his room. Everything was blank. Everything was a possibility.

Adam grew exited as he and Howard drew nearer to his old room. They made their way up the sweeping spiral staircase in the main hall, past the door to his Father's room. He turned the knob and was surprised to find it unlocked. He was thinking about how odd this was when he noticed a young, sandy haired, man standing in the middle of his room. The unexpected presence of another person in the house was shock enough, but as soon as he got a good look at the man standing in front of him, Adam's shock deepened.

The man smiled and said, "Hello big brother. It's been a long time."

Chapter 6

There were several seconds of silence before Adam realized that his jaw was hanging open. Words kept coming to mind – It's good to see you, I've missed you, how has it been – but nothing was able to make its way out.

Finally, Adam said the only thing he could manage, "Jonathan."

"Hey, there it is," his brother said forcing a laugh. "I knew you'd get it eventually."

Adam tried to push out a laugh in response, but it ended up sounding more like he was clearing his throat. There were a few more moments of strained silence before he could manage to get something else out, "You've grown so much."

Jonathan let out a genuine laugh; "Time will do that to you."

He had always been tall, but Jonathan used to be skinny. Now he was tan and muscular with sharp features and warm eyes, nothing like when Adam saw him last. Though it had been years since he and Jonathan had been in the same room, longer in fact than Adam and his Father had been estranged, the memories came flooding back as clear and familiar as if only a few days had passed.

Jonathan and Adam were close. They played together; they learned together, and they grew up together. There was only a year between them, but Adam took the role of older brother very seriously. He made sure Jonathan got his homework done. He made sure Jonathan had all his supplies before going to school. He made sure all the older boys were kind to Jonathan during baseball games. And Jonathan loved him for it.

Things began to change as the boys grew older. Adam was being given more and more responsibilities around the farm, and, as his responsibilities grew, his time for being a big brother diminished. Jonathan took it well at first, wanting to support his brother's success. But since he hardly knew what it was like to live life without Adam by his side, he soon began spending most of his days walking aimlessly around the farm. This lack of direction came to its head when the boys reached their late teens.

The memory was so burned in Adam's mind that he could recall every detail. It was a Thursday afternoon. He was in the barn, showing his Father a plan for a new kind of plow he had designed. The warmth of the sun was heating the sawdust, and filling the place with the smell of fresh cut wood. Adam and his Father were so focused on the plans that they hadn't heard Jonathan come in.

"Excuse me," Jonathan finally said once it was clear that they hadn't noticed him.

"Oh," Their Father gave a little surprised jump, "I'm sorry, son. I didn't see you there."

"I want my inheritance." Jonathan spoke flatly. It was only then that Adam noticed how strange his brother looked. His skin was slightly pale and covered in a fine layer of sweat. His breathing was sharp and irregular, and Adam thought he noticed a faint trembling.

"I'm sorry?" Their Father said with genuine

puzzlement.

"I want my inheritance, my share of the estate," he said, this time with more authority. "I've thought about it. I've had a lot of time to think about it, and there's no reason for me to stay here."

Adam stood stunned. Jonathan was clearly speaking to his Father, but Adam couldn't help but feel that every word was directed at him.

Jonathan continued, "I'm no farmer. I'm no good at working the vineyards, and I can't build anything to save my life. So I'd like my inheritance so that I can start something on my own."

Their Father looked at the ground, considering. Then he said, "Are you sure?"

But Jonathan interrupted him, his voice taking on a forced formal tone, "I just think I should seek my fortune elsewhere."

There was a long pause, and then their Father reached into his back pocket and pulled out his checkbook. Adam felt his face go numb. His hands went cold. He watched, frozen, as his Father wrote the largest check he had ever seen in his life and handed it to his little brother.

With nothing more than a curt, "Thank you," Jonathan turned on his heel and marched out of the barn. Adam stood, locked in mingled shock and confusion. When he could finally move, he ran out of the barn. He looked left and right for his brother, feeling panicked now, then ran toward the house. But before he could make it there, he saw Jonathan's car pulling out of the driveway and on to the main road.

Adam had called, of course. He even visited Jonathan in the city once. Jonathan smiled and joked as he always did, assuring that everything was fine, that this was just something he needed to do for himself. But their interaction felt like a pale imitation of remembered brotherly love. A wall had been built between them, and Adam was not sure how long it had been there.

There had been plenty of arguments between Adam and his Father, "Why did you let him go? Why did you give him the money?" These always ended with his Father giving the same answer, "Jonathan needs to find his way. It will do him no good if we find it for him."

It wasn't long before stories about Jonathan made

their way back to the house. Adam knew that something must be wrong once his brother stopped taking his calls. Before long he began hearing stories of elaborate and expensive parties, fast cars, and illicit substances. Eventually the stories became so painful to hear, that Adam stopped listening to them. That place in his heart his brother once held had finally frozen over. He never saw his brother again, at least not face to face, not until now.

Adam stared at Jonathan as he stood in his old bedroom. Jon looked just like the man that Adam had always imagined he would grow up to be. Despite the years of sorrow and pain his brother had caused, Adam could feel that old and cold part of his heart begin to warm again.

Without another word, Adam ran forward and wrapped his arms around his brother. Jonathan immediately returned the embrace, gripping tight. Both brothers began to shake as deep welling sobs came forth.

"I'm so sorry," Jonathan said in between sobs, "I'm so, so sorry."

Adam pulled away and held the sides of his brother's head so that he could look him in the eye, "No, Jon. I am the one who should be sorry. I'm the one who gave up on you. I'm the one who stopped being your brother. I stopped long before you did. I got so lost in trying to do well for Father, that I stopped being there for you."

A smile bloomed on Jonathan's face, the same infectious grin he'd had since they were young, "Well, we'll call it even then."

Adam felt a pang of guilt surge through him, "I'm sorry I didn't come to see you when you came back."

The smile on Jon's face widened, "Oh, come now, you still had things to work out. I knew even then it was more about you sorting things with Father than me."

Adam wiped the tears from his face, "I guess so."

"Go to him," Jonathan said. "We'll catch up afterward. It'll be easier to talk once everything is cleared."

"Where is He?" Adam asked.

"Oh, I think you know," his charismatic smile returned. "Where else would He be?"

Adam turned, knowing all at once where his Father

would be waiting. The spot … His favorite place in the house, and the place where everything had broken down. Howard stood in the doorway, beaming.

Adam had been so surprised by the sight of his brother that he had almost completely forgotten that the old caretaker was there, "Are you coming, Howard?"

"No, I think I'll stay here. The rest is for you and your Father."

Jonathan wrapped an arm around his brother, "I'll walk you down."

Chapter 7

Life changed after Jonathan left to "seek his fortune elsewhere." Once it became clear that his brother would not be returning, Adam lost himself in his work. Every waking moment was about making the farm run better. More efficiency, better training for his workers, higher yields on every harvest. These were the things that consumed him.

His Father maintained his cheery demeanor and deep interest in everything that Adam was doing, but His sadness was still apparent. Sometimes Adam would find Him upstairs staring out the window that overlooked the driveway, like He expected Jonathan to come back any moment. But he didn't, not for years.

Word of Jonathan's many exploits only caused Adam to dive even deeper into his work. Eventually news came that Jon's elaborate parties were losing some of their luster. It was clear that his inheritance, though vast, did have its limitations. Adam felt only a passing sense of pity. It was bound to happen eventually, after all.

It was a warm summer afternoon on the day it happened, the thing that tore Adam and his Father apart. Adam was out in the fields, checking on the progress of the wheat. He was focused on his work as usual. Jotting detailed notes about every acre on a notepad, when he noticed a man walking down the driveway. The man was dirty and thin. His skin had a pallid, sickly tone, and his tousled hair had been dyed three or four different shades of blue.

Adam thought the man looked vaguely familiar, but couldn't quite place him. Then the front door of the house burst open with a crash that made him jump. He turned and looked to see his Father come sprinting out of the house at full speed. He knocked over a potted plant as He leapt from the doorstep, but He didn't stop even as the pot shattered on the cobblestone. Father ran; his arms open wide, shouting something that Adam couldn't quite make out until he drew close.

"My son! My son! My Son has returned!" his Father

shouted over and over again at the top of His lungs.

With dawning understanding, Adam turned to look once more at the broken and disheveled man that was shuffling up the driveway. It was a pale and underfed facsimile of his younger brother, but there could be no question.

Father sprinted all the way down the drive, colliding with Jonathan so forcefully that they both nearly toppled over. But rather than falling, Father lifted Jon into the air in a great big bear hug. Howard came jogging just behind Father.

"Bring a shirt," Father said to the caretaker, "One of the nice ones."

Howard turned, but then Father called after him, "And find the biggest, fattest calf. I think we need to have a feast." He then pulled the ring off His finger and slipped it on Jonathan's, "Yes, a feast, because my son was dead and now he is alive again." Even from where he stood, Adam could see the tears rolling down his Father's face, "He was lost but now he is found."

"I was coming back to work for him," Jonathan's voice broke Adam out of the memory as they both made their way down the hall together.

"What?"

"I spent all the money," he said, lowering his head. "You must have known that. I didn't know you could spend that much money so fast," he gave a half-hearted laugh. "I lost my apartment, and all of my 'friends' left. I was up to my ears in debt. I was a junkie, I couldn't get a job."

Adam paused at the top of the stairs. He had never heard why his brother had decided to come home. He assumed that when the money ran out, Jonathan had come running back to Father to beg for more.

"I tried to find work for months," Jon continued. "Finally I managed to get something under the table at a pig farm. I only got paid a few bucks an hour to feed the pigs. I knew things were bad when the pig slop started looking tasty." He gave another pathetic laugh, "I figured that Dad's workers have it fifty times better than this. All of them can put food on their own tables."

Adam rested a hand on his brother's back, "I didn't know."

"I was too ashamed to come back, but I might not have made it otherwise. I had this whole speech planned about how He didn't need to treat me as a son anymore, that I'd be happy to be treated just as one of His workers." A fresh tear rolled down Jonathan's face, "But I didn't get a chance to say that speech. Dad grabbed me and squeezed the air out of me. Before I could speak, there was a ring on my finger, and I was being changed into fresh clothes."

Adam remained silent, not knowing what to say.

"I know you left just after I came back, and I think I know why." With that smile again, "I just want you to know that it's okay. I had to run away for a while to get my head on straight. I don't hold it against you for doing the same."

Adam smiled and looked down the stairs, "I guess that leaves only one more thing to fix."

"Go to Him, Adam. I'll see you after."

Memory came flooding back as Adam descended the stairs, unbidden and unstoppable, but not as unwanted as it used to be. It was as if he was walking to go relive that terrible moment again, that moment when the connection between him and his Father broke.

Adam hadn't returned from the fields upon Jonathan's return. He had been so surprised, not only by his brother's sudden appearance, but also his Father's dramatic response to it. So much effort had been put toward stuffing the emotions that his brother's departure and debauchery had caused, that Adam didn't know what to do with them as they welled up one after the other. He was glad. There was no doubt about that. Of course he was glad his brother had come back. He could have died or been forever lost in some drug induced stupor. But Adam was also angry. Angry at his brother for leaving, angry at his Father for being so immediately forgiving, and angry at himself for being so angry. There was sadness too, but he couldn't figure out why.

It was near sunset when he finally started making his way back home from the fields. He could hear the sound of celebration long before he was near the door. He hesitated at the front door for a long moment, not sure whether to smile or frown as he entered. Finally he decided that he would go in around back.

The sun was setting when he stepped on the back

porch, the spot, his favorite spot. He stood there, telling himself that he wanted to watch the sun go down before going inside, but knowing that there was another reason.

"There you are, Adam." Howard's voice came from behind. "I hadn't seen you. Did you know that your brother…"

"Yes, I saw him," Adam interrupted, trying to keep the mixed emotions out of his voice. "I'll be in soon, I just want to watch the sunset."

"Very well," the old caretaker responded, not at all convinced.

The sounds of the party grew momentarily louder as Howard opened the door to enter. This only served to anger Adam further. A party! Really? Your son throws away his entire inheritance and the first thing You do is throw him a party.

"Hello son." The sudden sound of his Father's voice made him jump.

He turned, "Hello Father."

"Is there something wrong?"

The patient tone, and polite questioning only made Adam's blood boil.

"Look!" Adam said, jabbing his finger at his Father, "All these years I've been slaving for You, and never once disobeyed You, and You've never given me anything close to a party like that." This was not entirely true, and Adam knew it. But the anger was beginning to cloud his mind, "And now Your son squandered Your money on who knows what, and the first thing You do is throw him a party?"

His Father frowned, clearly hurt, "You are always with me, Adam. Everything I have is yours, everything."

"So You just want me to take it and throw it all away! Well I'm not like that. I've tried to expand Your fields, make You richer. I've worked day in and day out to do great things for You. And now You celebrate when he comes home to get more of what he wasted?"

"We have to celebrate, Adam. Your brother was dead, but now he is alive. He was lost, but now he is found!"

Still the cloud in Adam's mind darkened. Hardly thinking about what he was doing, he reached into his pocket and pulled out the key to his Father's house, the handmade key that his Father had forged with a little eagle figure at the top.

"Well, I'm glad, Father, I'm glad You got Your son back. At least You'll have one." Then he threw the key over the edge of the deck where it clattered against the cliff and fell into the ocean.

The memory returned again and again as he walked down the stairs, playing through his mind like a song stuck on repeat. His Father had called out to him as he stomped off, but Adam didn't listen.

Though the pain was still there, he didn't see the memory the way he had for all those years. Anytime the memory had come to him before, he viewed it through a red cloud of anger. Now it only made him sad. For the first time Adam realized how much he had thrown away with that key. He fingered the eagle key on the ring of keys that Howard had given him. It was time to put an end to all the sadness and anger. It was time to let it go once and for all. With a deep breath, Adam stepped down the last step, and walked through the door to the porch where his Father was waiting.

Chapter 8

Adam felt like he was stepping right back into that day so many years ago. The sun was beginning to set, and the view was as perfect and breathtaking as it was the last time he and his Father stood here. Father stood with an expression as bright as the sun setting behind Him.

"Hello Adam."

"Hello Father. How I've missed you," the kindness in His voice could be matched only by the kindness in His eyes. "It has been far too long!"

His Father stepped forward, arms open, and wrapped him in a loving embrace. Adam shrank back, more from surprise at the sudden contact than anything else.

"It's alright, son. I'm just glad you're here."

Father held him against His chest, so tight that Adam could hear the sound of His heartbeat. Simple as it was, he felt as though the embrace was nurturing him, feeding his soul.

"I'm sorry," the words leapt suddenly from his mouth, but they were true, "I'm so sorry."

"That's alright," He said with a smile. "You showed up, and sometimes that's all it takes."

Adam made himself smile. It was not as difficult as he expected.

"You've let me show you quite a lot today, and for that I'm grateful." He let go of Adam with one hand, but held him tightly with the other, "But I have to ask you to indulge me just a bit further, because I have a few more things to say."

Adam nodded.

His Father smiled, and then continued, "You are my son, Adam. You always have been and you always will be. I know that I have a great many children. In fact, I've never met anyone that is not my child. But that doesn't mean I love you less than any of them. That's why I do things the way that I do, because you knowing my love for you, is the most important thing to me, and true love has to be shown."

Though he was a grown man now, it was amazing how being near his Father like this made him feel as he always had, as a child. It was wonderful!

"Now there's risk in showing something rather than saying it." His Father continued, "In fact a great risk! What if people see what you're showing, but misunderstand it? Or what if they won't look at all? I've been trying to show you how much I care for you, and you have been refusing to see for some time now. But there's nothing quite like seeing the light in someone's eyes when they find what you've hidden for them. Nothing like it! So I take the risk! I take the chance my affections may go unnoticed, because it is worth the risk, and I trust my children." He pointed at the key in Adam's hand, "Do you know why I put an eagle on the top of your key?"

Adam shook his head.

"Because you've got eyes as an eagle, son. You see what no one else can. You see what's in the distance and the path to get there. That's why I put you in charge of my fields. I knew you'd make them great."

"Why didn't I get a party?" Adam realized how childish it sounded, knew it was silly. But it came out all the same.

His Father smiled, "That is the question, isn't it? Why didn't I get a party? Why won't people come to my shop? Why did she leave me? Why can't I pay all the bills?"

Each question sent a pang through Adam's chest.

"I put a lot of thought into the conversation we had the night you left. I was completely baffled by the idea you thought I wouldn't throw you a party. I know you were upset. Everyone says things they don't mean when they're upset, but those words usually point to the things they really do mean. You see Jonathan squandered his inheritance. That you know! He spent it on everything he thought would make him feel better about himself, everything that he hoped would fill the hole he felt in his heart. What you may not know is that you squandered your inheritance just as much as Jon did."

Adam was surprised at this. He had always been the most frugal person he knew. He even made the decorations for the grand opening at his business just to save a few dollars.

His Father answered the question written on his face, "You squandered your inheritance by letting it sit there."

There were a few seconds of silence, enough time for the idea to sink in.

"I meant what I said last time we stood on this deck together, Adam. 'Everything I have is yours!' That is true and always has been true. Everything I own became your property the day you were born into my household. You could always take as much or as little of it as you like. Jon took more than he was ready to handle, and it brought him nothing but pain. It has been equally painful for you to deny your inheritance, fighting to prove you don't need it, or you're above it. I don't know when you decided you needed to work to gain my affections or prove your worth, but that has never been true. I've adored you since before you knew what work was."

A warmth spread through Adam's stomach, a great gleaming glow. It was warmth he had known everyday as a child, but had been lost when he left. He thought that this feeling had died after he left his

Father, yet here it was, just as bright and new as it had been. In the distance he thought he heard music, then voices. Then he realized that these sounds weren't in his head, they were getting closer and growing louder.

"What's that sound?" Adam asked.

"Ah yes," His Father said, releasing his embrace and stepping toward the door to the house, "You have followed my every invitation as you have made your way through this house. Now I have one last invitation to give. Your brother squandered his inheritance because he didn't know how to manage it. You squandered your inheritance because you let it go to waste. What is the answer then? How much do you need to take, and how much should you leave. When are you ready for more? How do you get ready for more?"

Adam could feel anticipation swelling in his chest.

"Well, my boy, I can't tell you. It's too beautiful for that. So, once again, I must show you. I'm ready to show you the answer to these and every other question like them. All you have to do is stay close to me and I will show you."

Adam smiled, the warmth in his chest filling every

inch of his body. The music and sound of people grew even louder.

"What is that sound?" He asked again.

His Father laughed, "I almost forgot. That is your party. My son was dead, but he is alive again. He was lost, but now he is found. At the beginning of this journey I told you I had a gift for you. Here it is," He said gesturing toward the door to his house. "Come in and let me show the abundance I have for you. I've waited far too long," as his Father extended his hand to him.

There were still so many questions. There were still places of pain in Adam's heart. But somehow all that didn't matter so much anymore. Maybe his business could be saved, or maybe it couldn't, even that wasn't as important anymore. All that mattered was he was with his Father again. So much of his energy had been sunk into keeping his business afloat, and blocking out the pain he had been feeling. It had been a long time since he had felt this light. Life had been aimless, now he knew the direction he had to start going.

"All right, Dad. Let's see what you can do." Then Adam stepped forward into his Father's embrace again, the warmth filling his mind and heart.

Together they stepped into the place they both, once again, called home.

Appendix I

OUR HEAVENLY FATHER HAS GIVEN US KEYS FOR OUR JOURNEY

> *"To the angel of the Church in Philadelphia He wrote: These are the words of him who is holy and true, who holds the key of David. What he opens no one can shut, and what he shuts no one can open. I know your deeds. See, I have placed before you an open door that no one can shut"* (Revelation 3:7 & 8a - NIV).

Notice how Jesus is described here in verse seven. He is described as the "Keeper of the keys."

Jesus is the Keeper of the keys. He has the key to every circumstance in your life. You don't have to know key men if you know the Keeper of the keys!

There are Keys throughout the Bible:

- The Key to the House of David (Isaiah 22:22).
- The Key of Knowledge (Luke 11:52).
- Keys to the Kingdom (Matthew 16:19).
- The Keys to Hell and Death (Revelation 1:18).
- The Key to Open Doors (Revelation 3:7)
- The Key to the Bottomless Pit (Revelation 20:1).

What is a Key?

- A metal instrument, usually of a specifically contoured shape, that is made to fit a lock, and when rotated, operates the lock's mechanism, a means of achieving a desired end such as the "key" to happiness.

Keys are incredibly small, but give access to great power. A key that weighs less than three ounces can open a two ton steel door. A small and simple key activates all the power held within a twelve-cylinder engine. Keys are a powerful picture of how a simple truth can be the difference between free access and no access to God's Kingdom.

The Kingdom of God is principle based. The

blessings of God are available for those sons and daughters who are willing to dig deep into the Word of God. Just as a miner digs for gold, the child of God will find Golden Nuggets of wisdom that will lead him or her to a life of *supernatural abundance*, but only if they are willing to find the keys!

Living from *supernatural abundance* is unlocked by divine principles. These principles are like keys that open doors. When you are without a key, success becomes a struggle. A keyless man is a hopeless man.

> *"For he said, Unto you it is given to know the secrets of the Kingdom of God"* (Luke 8:10).

> *"It is the glory of God to conceal a thing: but the honour of kings is to search out a matter"* (Proverb 25:2).

Our God is an extravagant Dad Who desires for His children to walk in Supernatural Abundance

In the Old Testament there is a story that gives us an insight as to how much of Father's extravagant love is available to us. God uses David as a living illustration of what grace and abundance is all about. I want to point out some observations about amazing grace. In 2 Samuel 9 we read the story of David and

Mephibosheth:

"David asked, 'Is there anyone still left of the house of Saul to whom I can show kindness for Jonathan's sake?' Now there was a servant of Saul's household named Ziba. They summoned him to appear before David, and the king said to him, 'Are you Ziba?' 'At your service,' he replied. The king asked, 'Is there no one still alive from the house of Saul to whom I can show God's kindness?' Ziba answered the king, 'There is still a son of Jonathan; he is lame in both feet.' 'Where is he?' the king asked. Ziba answered, 'He is at the house of Makir son of Ammiel in Lo Debar.' So King David had him brought from Lo Debar, from the house of Makir, son of Ammiel. When Mephibosheth son of Jonathan, the son of Saul, came to David, he bowed down to pay him honor. David said, 'Mephibosheth! 'At your service,' he replied. 'Don't be afraid,' David said to him, 'for I will surely show you kindness for the sake of your Father Jonathan. I will restore to you all the land that belonged to your

grandfather Saul, and you will always eat at my table.' Mephibosheth bowed down and said, "What is your servant, that you should notice a dead dog like me?" (NIV).

The text focuses on two main characters: David and Mephibosheth, the grandson of Saul and the son of Jonathan. It is a story about distress that is experienced, caused by change. It is a story about an invitation that was accepted. It is a story about friendship, promises, grace, love, compassion, forgiveness, and hope.

David is generally thought of as the little shepherd who slew the giant, committed adultery with Bathsheba, or ran from Saul. But we remember him for being "a man after God's own heart," relocating the Ark of the Covenant to Jerusalem, as well as his friendship with Jonathan, the son of Saul. It is this friendship with Jonathan that shows us a picture of amazing grace.

A Bond that Cannot be Broken

In the book of Samuel, we see a very beautiful friendship between Jonathan and David. We know that they were very close. Scripture gives us insight into the love they had for each other as if it were their own souls. David and Jonathan had bonded together and were very loyal to one another in spite of how Saul felt about David. David and Jonathan had made a covenant of friendship to one another promising whoever survived or outlived the other they would look after their family. This incident certainly stands as a challenge as to how we should "do life" with our friends. It should remind us of promises we've made, kept, and/or broke. It is also a challenge to honor the promises made to our parents, grandparents, and descendants, and to do so reflects how we keep our promises to God.

During a time of much turmoil, Saul had failed as the first king, and David had become king. Jonathan and Saul died during the same battle on Mount Gilboa, leaving five year old Mephibosheth, Jonathan's son, without a father or grandfather. During the skirmish, the nurse picks up the young child and runs toward safety. While running for their lives, she drops Mephibosheth. She saves his life, but now he is crippled for life. It was a time of chaos. In one day the king is dead, the prince is dead, and Mephibosheth is running for his life.

During that period of time, most kings tried to completely destroy the families of their rivals in order to prevent any of the descendants from rising up and trying to regain the throne. David didn't do that. He actively sought the descendants of his covenant friend, Jonathan. David was told that Jonathan had a son that was alive, but lame.

Mephibosheth belonged to the royal line, and thus lived in exile and fear far from King David. He was subject to persecution and slander. But because David was a son of covenant, he rescued Mephibosheth due to a promise that he made to his father. David honored his covenant to Jonathan, even though Mephibosheth had never heard about the promise.

King David's search landed his servants in Lodebar, a city east of the Jordan River. Lodebar was a city characterized by its barrenness, wastelands, and devastation. It was a city in the midst of the wilderness. Lodebar was a place with no pastures, or no greenery. It was desolate!

In Lodebar, Mephibosheth lost his rank, lost his prestige, lost his respectability, lost his reputation, lost his superiority, and lost his self-will. In Lodebar, Mephibosheth went from living in the palace, to hiding out with a family friend in a desolate place. Mephibosheth went from being the prince to being a servant. Mephibosheth went from powerful to fearful.

When Mephibosheth, whose name means, "he scatters shame" or "destroying shame," came face to face with David at twenty years old, he fell flat on the floor in an act of submission. He referred to himself as a dead dog; meaning he felt like he had no worth or value. During that time dogs were not held in such high regard as they are today. Dogs didn't have their own houses, clothes, doctors, food, and the like. At that time dogs were actually disliked and held in contempt. He was comparing himself to something very low and helpless.

Mephibosheth was in fear for his life. He really didn't know how things were going to work out. All he knew was that kings had a way of destroying the remnants of the previous king's family. Mephibosheth humbled himself, fell on his face, reverenced the King, and confessed his unworthiness. David quickly put Mephibosheth at ease, offered forgiveness, and invited him to dine at the King's table. David cared for Mephibosheth the rest of his natural life. He was accepted and adopted into the royal family. David took him to the throne and gave back everything that had been taken from him.

When Mephibosheth came to David, he did not get what he thought he deserved. He received grace. When he received grace, he also received more blessings than he could have ever imagined. Grace was expanded. Notice what grace provided for Mephibosheth, and what Father God's saving grace provides for you and me.

Grace Provided A Future – In Lodebar, Mephibosheth had nothing. He was poor. He was an outcast. He was a fugitive. He had no hope and no prospects for his future. All he had was a pair of crutches and little else. But, when he met grace, everything changed! All of his needs were met and his future was secured. Grace gave him something he never could have had in Lodebar: grace gave him a future. Grace gave him the abundance of the King!

Grace Provided A Family – Mephibosheth was adopted out of Saul's family and into David's. Grace gave him something he did not have before it was extended to him. Grace gave him a family! Every day he lived, Mephibosheth was reminded by his surroundings, and by the presence of the King, he was the recipient of grace. He was where he was because of the grace of the King!

Grace Provided Fulfilllment – Mephibosheth was "a nobody" in a house full of somebodies. There was Absalom, perfect and handsome. There were also David's other sons. There were David's beautiful wives and daughters. There was Joab, the general, proud and strong. There were princes and princesses, soldiers and statesmen, men of wealth, and men of power. All of these took their place at the table of King David. As the family gathered, there was the sound of a crippled man coming down the hallway. There was the clump of crutches and the sound of his feet being dragged. It was Mephibosheth, and he took his place at the King's table with all the rights and privileges as the rest. Then, when he took his seat and the tablecloth fell across his legs; he looked just like the rest. Grace took "a nobody" from nowhere, and made him a child of the King!

David's love was exemplary of the love of Daddy God. It came out of a merciful heart. He didn't have to find Jonathan's son. Nobody else was there when he made the covenant. Nobody but David knew what he had promised. Nobody would have even cared. Since Saul had tried to kill David twenty-three times, no one would have blamed David if he hadn't kept his part of the promise. No one would have known, but David. David was noble, gracious and sought out the undeserving lad and gave him all that was his. Only God can touch a man and make him do this kind of deed. Mephibosheth was lifted from poverty to abundance through the grace of the King.

Your Dad wants You to Sit at the King's Table

Our God is a God of abundance. Everything He does, He does to "increase," not "decrease." A God of "fullness," not "emptiness." He's a loving Father who wants His kids to enjoy the blessings and benefits of all He has for them. Being a child of God is not just knowing that heaven is in your future, but it's also knowing that heaven and life abundant is here and now.

If this is true, then why are so many believers living in lack? As I travel around the world I wonder, *Where is the increase, where is the supernatural abundance God's kids should be enjoying?*

Jesus declared in John 10:10:

> *"The thief cometh not, but for to steal,*
> *and to kill, and to destroy: I am come that*
> *they might have life, and that they might*
> *have it more abundantly."*

Jesus stated His purpose for His kids is that we might not only know "life," but we would know a quality of life that He called "abundant living!" A life full of meaning, purpose, and void of fear.

The journey to *supernatural abundance* begins when

you believe God truly wants you to live an abundant life. The first step is knowing His grace is more than sufficient to transform your life. The rest comes with the journey.

ATTITUDE DEFINED

Attitude can be defined as "a mental filter through which we process our thoughts and view the world." Given the fact that the average person has more than 50,000 separate thoughts per day, it's obvious that the expression "attitude is everything" is true.

There are many people who filter their thoughts through a negative screen, which leads them to view the world as a dark, ominous place populated with gloom and doom. When we filter those same thoughts through the screen of a positive attitude, the world is a bright adventure overflowing with surprises and abundance.

After all, who wants to be around someone who sees the glass half-empty instead of half-full? A bad attitude is like a virus, it spreads to everyone around you. Just like a cold germ, every time the bad attitude opens its mouth, more people are infected.

There are some things in life we can't do anything about. Where we were born, who our parents were, and what we look like. One thing we can do something about is our attitude. Nobody can *make* us have a good attitude or a bad one; it's a choice.

Good versus a Bad Attitude

- A bad attitude will always blame others when things go wrong: A good attitude will accept responsibility for making mistakes.

- A bad attitude makes excuses: a good attitude gets results. A bad attitude says, "*Get going!*" A good attitude says, "*Let's get going.*"

- A bad attitude looks at life as a trial to endure. A good attitude looks at life as an adventure to enjoy.

- A bad attitude looks at a rose bush and sees the thorns. A good attitude looks past the thorns and sees the roses.

I'm sure you could add to this list. But I want to ask you a question: which person would you prefer to be, the one with a good attitude, or the one with a bad attitude? Would you rather be known as someone who lights up a room when you enter the room, or when you leave the room? Let's face it, we love being around positive people because their attitude is contagious, and we want to catch it. No doubt about it, people with great attitudes light up a room when they enter it, not when they leave it."

Attitude is the Key Ingredient to Successful Living

We are in charge of our own attitudes. We can face change with a negative attitude (the glass half empty) or we can choose to face change with a positive attitude (the glass half-full). I have come to believe that attitude is more important than facts, my past, my failures, my successes, or what other people think, say, or do. Attitude has the power to make or break your organization, your Church, or your home.

Some people have such a rotten attitude that they think the whole world stinks. Ninety-five times out of one hundred, when we begin to feel that things in life stinks, the problem is not with the world or with others. The problem is with us. Our attitude has become negative. When you change a negative attitude to a positive one, you can change your world.

Warren Wiersbe, former pastor of Moody Memorial Church in Chicago wrote: "Without a doubt the human mind is the most awesome creation of God. With it, God has given us the ability to think, to reason and to choose whether we will focus on positive thoughts or negative thoughts. In every one of our lives, there is the positive and the negative. The choice as to which one we will focus on, feed on, and nurture on is up to us."

Model the Attitude of Jesus

The greatest leader who ever lived had the greatest attitude! His name was Jesus.

We would expect history's greatest leader to have the greatest attitude. Paul said, *"Let this mind be in you that was also in Christ Jesus."* All we have to do is watch Jesus' actions, listen to His words, and we will understand that He was the master of His own attitude. Hebrews 12:2 says we are to, *"Look unto Jesus, the author and finisher of our faith, who for the joy set before Him endured the cross, despising the shame, and has sat down at the right hand of the throne of God."*

Three Key Facets of Jesus' Winning Attitude:

1. Jesus knew why He was here.

He wasn't confused about His purpose. Jesus was very sure as to why He was here, what He was to do, and who sent Him. If we believe we are here for a purpose, we will live in the present moment of divine destiny. We will not wander, be confused, or live with negativity or doubt.

The enemy tries to convince us that we are the only person ever born without purpose. It's a lie. Call it a lie. Believe it's a lie. Then start to live like it's a lie! God has a purpose for every son and daughter of His!

2. Jesus knew what He was sent to do.

He was clear about His mission. Knowing we have a purpose is only the first step in defining that purpose. There has to be a "why" attached to it. Again, Jesus is very clear. Look at Jesus' "I am come" statements:

- "To fulfilll the law" (Matthew 5:17).
- "To bring a sword" (Matthew 10:34).
- "To send fire on the Earth" (Luke 12:49).
- "To give sight to the blind" (John 9:39).
- "To bring light to the world" (John 12:46).

- "To seek and save the lost" (Luke 19:10).

Jesus defined His mission statement, even without the proliferation of "how-to" books today, "*I am come that they might have life, and that they might have it more abundantly*" (John 10:10).

3. Jesus knew where He was going.

He was sure of His destiny. The one thing the enemy hated about Jesus was the fact that Jesus knew His destiny. The Devil tried to do all he could to stop Jesus. Jesus' experience in the wilderness was about Satan's attempts to detour His destiny.

Jesus expressed His destiny in the "*I go*" statements:

- "*And then I go unto him that sent me*" (John 7:33).
- "*For I know whence I came, and where I go*" (John 8:44).
- "*I go to prepare a place for you*" (John 14:2-3).
- "*I must needs go through Samaria*" (John 4:4).

No wonder Jesus had such a great attitude. No wonder the enemy wants to kill *your* attitude. When we look at the life of Jesus, we can see why there was so much pressure on Him. Men and women who know their purpose, mission, and destiny cannot be stopped!

To have the attitude of Jesus is to think right, speak right, and to act according to God's word. When we make a conscious choice to do these three things, we can be assured the promise of prosperity will be given without hesitation or restriction.

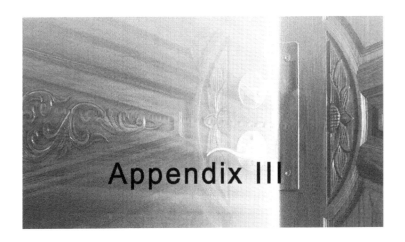

OVERCOMING A SPIRIT OF POVERTY

Don't Settle for Less than Your Father Intends

The Bible teaches there is a spirit opposite to abundance, and it's called the spirit of lack and poverty. Many of God's children live far below what their heavenly Father intended for them.

It's much like a story I heard of a young man who immigrated to the United States many years ago. He saved up enough money to buy passage and boarded a ship to follow the American dream. He knew he had enough money to pay for his fare, but not enough to buy food or sustain him on the trip. He packed all the provisions he could carry, but he knew it wouldn't be enough for the entire journey. About two days into the trip, the man looked at the few bits of cheese and crackers that remained and thought, *Well, I guess I can make it the rest of the way without food.*

While the man sat on the upper deck looking out at the ocean, a steward walked by and said, *"Young man, it's lunchtime. Why don't you come and join us in the dining room?"* The young man said, *"Sir, I only had enough money for passage. I don't have enough money to pay for food."* The steward said, *"Let me see your ticket."* The steward looked at the man's ticket and said, *"This ticket is a full fare ticket which entitles you to lodging, food, and every amenity the ship offers!"*

This young man had the mentality that is too common among believers today. He was willing to go without food to pursue his dream, though in fact, he was entitled to everything the ship had to offer. You may think, *hat a tragedy!* But there are many people that live their entire lives like this young man.

Let me share with you some thoughts about the spirit of poverty and what wealth and abundance really means.

There is a scripture that describes what I'm talking about:

"Whoever disregards discipline comes to poverty and shame, but whoever heeds correction is honored" (Proverbs 13:18 - NIV).

Someone asked me, *"What is an idol?"* The best definition I've ever read is: anything you have to check with before obeying the instructions of the Holy Spirit. When we live in the cycle of "insufficiency," we will many times say *"NO"* to Holy Spirit! The spirit of poverty must be exposed before it can ever be broken.

I want to break down the individual links in the chain of poverty for you. Before I do, it would be helpful to define terms that are often discussed in the body of Christ:

* Riches
* Wealth
* Prosperity
* Abundance

Riches or Wealth:

"And you shall remember the LORD your God, for it is He who gives you power to get wealth that He may establish His covenant which He swore

to your fathers, as it is this day"
(Deuteronomy 8:18).

When speaking of the word wealth, some only view it in terms of money. This is a great deception. Money is only a part of true wealth. In my life I have seen many people who have a great deal of money, but I would not consider them truly wealthy.

When using these two words "riches or wealth," we are speaking about considerable financial or material assets. There is more than having large bank accounts or owning large estates. I'm sure you have met people just like I described. They have many "things," but that does not equal wealth.

My definition of wealth may be a little different from yours. I believe that wealth is: being provided for through an unlimited supply. Philippians 4:19 says:

> *"And my God shall supply all of your need according to His riches in glory by Christ Jesus."*

We need to understand! Wealth must be viewed in light of present need. For example, money may not be the present need. The need may be healing for a family member, peace of mind, a new job, or help for a rebellious child. Financial wealth is not the end in itself. God's ultimate will for us is that we be made whole.

> *"Measure wealth not by the things you have, but by the things you have for which you would not take money."*
> ~Anonymous

Did you know the most famous gold strike in American history occurred in January 1848 when a man named John Marshall found gold at Sutter's Mill in northern California? The find set off a gold rush that reached a frenzied pitch. It even attracted prospectors from Europe. But it ruined Marshall and John Stutter; the man who owned the land where gold laid for the taking. Gold seekers overran Sutter's land, his cattle were stolen, and he was driven into bankruptcy. Marshall died drunken and penniless.

What is Prosperity and Abundance?

I'm linking two words together to help you understand what I mean when I talk about prosperity and abundance.

When using these two words, it does not necessarily mean that a person has much money in the bank, or owns great material possessions. The promise from God is that *all* your needs will be met and there will be enough left over to share.

In short, when we think in terms of God's provision, we are not necessarily talking about people whom others would consider to be very wealthy or rich. I would like to think it means succeeding in what each individual is called and commissioned to do. There is an old saying that goes like this, "*Where God guides ... He provides.*"

The apostle John said:

> "*Beloved, I pray that you may prosper in all things and be in health, just as your soul prospers*" (3 John 1:2).

If you study John's third epistle, you will discover that he was writing under the inspiration of the Holy Spirit. He was telling us that God wants us to "prosper" in all things, and be in "health" just as our "soul prospers." This covers every area of life, including the material.

John, in using the word "prosper," is saying, "to

have a prosperous or successful journey, or accomplish what you intend to with success." It's the same word that Paul used in Romans 1:10 when he prayed he may have a "prosperous journey by the will of God" to visit and minister to the Christians at Rome.

There are many people who would not consider Paul very successful, and certainly not prosperous. I can tell you this; God had a different view than most people concerning the ministry of Paul.

In order to get to Rome, his destination, Paul endured hardship, suffering, and fear. After the trauma of shipwreck (remember God told him no one would suffer loss), being thrown onto an island as a castaway, and being bit by a viper, Paul was witness to the supernatural power of God. That which appeared to be disaster, God used for His glory when a revival exploded and many were saved and healed.

Paul made it to Rome and had a prosperous journey. But I can guarantee it was not comfortable or luxurious. It was prosperous because he accomplished the purpose of God!

I have received many insights on abundance. From

studying scripture, abundance to me means having all that's needed, plus something to spare or left over to share with others. Walking in abundance lifts you out of your own needs and puts you in the cycle where you receive from your Father, and generously turn and meet someone else's need.

What is the Spirit of Poverty?

Poverty is not living in a ghetto or growing up in the most rundown part of town. Being poor does not come as a result of high unemployment or the lack of qualifying skills. These are the "fruits" of poverty, not the "roots" of poverty.

Being broke is a temporary condition. I believe that poverty is a "spirit" right out of the pit of hell. I'm sure there have been times when you had a shortage of money. That does not necessarily mean you have a spirit of poverty.

Poverty is a destructive spirit that robs people of their dreams, goals, motivations, and desires. I'm sure you have heard the phrase "poverty stricken." This alludes to the concept that poverty is something that comes upon a person, a family, a community, or a nation.

Poverty is most often connected with un-righteousness. In scripture it was the "unrighteousness" of an individual, or nation as a whole, that brought poverty upon the people of God.

The widow of Zarephath in 1 Kings 17:8–16 is a prime example of living in poverty as a result of God's judgment upon the rule of Ahab.

> *"Then the word of the LORD came to him, saying, 'Arise, go to Zarephath, which belongs to Sidon, and dwell there. See, I have commanded a widow there to provide for you.' So he arose and went to Zarephath. And when he came to the gate of the city, indeed a widow was there gathering sticks. And he called to her and said, 'Please bring me a little water in a cup, that I may drink.' And as she was going to get it, he called to her and said, 'Please bring me a morsel of bread in your hand.'*
>
> *So she said, 'As the LORD your God lives, I do not have bread, only a handful of flour in a bin, and a little oil in a jar; and see, I am gathering a couple of sticks*

that I may go in and prepare it for myself and my son, that we may eat it, and die.'

And Elijah said to her, 'Do not fear; go and do as you have said, but make me a small cake from it first, and bring it to me; and afterward make some for yourself and your son. For thus says the LORD God of Israel: 'The bin of flour shall not be used up, nor shall the jar of oil run dry, until the day the LORD sends rain on the Earth.'

So she went away and did according to the word of Elijah; and she and he and her household ate for many days. The bin of flour was not used up, nor did the jar of oil run dry, according to the word of the LORD, which He spoke by Elijah."

While it is unfortunate that the widow got caught up in the midst of the king's disobedience (and God did take care of her through the miracle that she witnessed), nevertheless spiritual bankruptcy led to physical judgment.

There seems to be one question that must be asked,

and it is this: why haven't all the social programs eradicated poverty? Why is it that America, for example, has spent billions and billions of dollars all over the world in aid to help eliminate poverty, but some of those same countries are poorer today than ever before? No one can dispute the fact that poverty is rampant all over the world. I believe the problem goes beyond environment. There is a spirit involved! If the spirit of poverty is ever exposed, then the liberating power of the gospel can penetrate and bring hope, healing, and prosperity.

The spirit of poverty is a chain around the neck of many individuals, families, and Churches.

Identifying the Links of the Chain of Poverty

Let's look at the chain, and let me expose seven links that are major signs of poverty:

1. Refusing Instruction.

> *"Whoever disregards discipline comes to poverty and shame, but whoever heeds correction is honored"* (Proverbs 13:18 - NIV).

God has given certain instructions to help people

break the chain of poverty. People have trouble breaking free because they don't read God's instruction manual, the Bible.

God's people act like the proverbial parent who buys toys for their children on Christmas and tries to put together those toys without reading the instructions. The truth of the matter is, it's always best to read the instruction manual if you want to do the job right.

"Moreover all these curses shall come upon thee, and shall pursue thee, and overtake thee, till thou be destroyed; because thou hearkenedst not unto the voice of the LORD thy God, to keep his commandments and his statutes which he commanded thee: And they shall be upon thee for a sign and for a wonder, and upon thy seed for ever. Because thou servedst not the LORD thy God with joyfulness, and with gladness of heart, for the abundance of all things; Therefore shalt thou serve thine enemies which the LORD shall send against thee, in hunger, and in thirst, and in nakedness, and in want of all things: and he shall put a yoke of iron upon thy neck, until he have destroyed thee" (Deuteronomy 28:45-48).

Many people make the mistake of judging themselves by their intentions and other people by their actions. In doing this, they forget that the road to poverty, divorce, and death are paved with good intentions. One must realize that a good intention is actually the voice of the Holy Spirit communicating to our spirit the will of God in a certain situation. Our spirit then communicates with our intellect. Our intellect agrees that the instruction it has received from the Spirit is the right way to act in order to illuminate God's character to a world that is seeking workable truth.

In the book of James he declared, *"But prove yourselves doers of the word, and not merely hearers who delude themselves"* (James 1:22 - NASB). We do not, however, deceive those who we are trying to convince that the way of God is a better way of life than anything the world can offer.

Instruction or knowledge can only benefit us when we are willing to act upon it. I have met many so-called "wise men" that are poor and wretched. In their own mind they truly believe that they are legendary. Yet, they have very little or no fruit within their lives to back up their so called wisdom.

Unless the believer acts in faith on the word of God, he cannot justly hold back the thieves of abundance.

Please understand, curses don't come to teach you a lesson. Curses come because people refuse to listen to the word of God and obey the instructions of the book! The law of traffic control says there is a way to drive that is very safe. Stop at the red light and drive on through the green light. If you choose to do it another way, it's not the fault of the city if you get a ticket for breaking the law.

Curses are very real and can affect our lives. Curses come for a reason as stated in Proverbs 26:2 - NKJV:

> *"Like a flitting sparrow, like a flying swallow, so a curse without cause shall not alight."*

Just as a bird alights on its appointed place because it has a right to be there, so a curse alights upon us for a cause. If a curse comes, there is a reason for it.

> *"But it shall come to pass, if you do not obey the voice of the Lord your God, to observe carefully all His commandments and His statutes which I command you today, that all these curses will come upon you and overtake you"* (Deuteronomy 28:15 - NKJV).

Be careful not to place your faith in the world system and doubt the Word of God. You will end up doubting your beliefs, and believing your doubts. Lack of knowledge causes failure:

> *"My People are destroyed for lack of knowledge"* (Hosea: 4:6a - NKJV).

The open door that allows curses to come is disobedience. Blessings come through listening to the word of God, and then doing the word of God. To walk in fullness is to obey! To live under a curse is to disobey!

There are a total of 53 verses that discuss curses. Some of the curses mentioned are:

- Mental and emotional curses
- Physical curses
- Relational curses
- Oppression
- Failure
- Lack
- Defeat

But God has a way out of poverty. God states His will this way:

"Now it shall come to pass, if you diligently obey the voice of the Lord your God, to observe carefully all His commandments which I command you today, that the Lord your God will set you high above all nations of the Earth. And all these blessings shall come upon you and overtake you, because you obey the voice of the Lord your God" (Deuteronomy 28:1-2 - NKJV).

Take time to read Deuteronomy 28. Its true, all of the many blessings God outlines in this Scripture are for you and for anyone who will obey His word. Meditate on them and rejoice:

- Exaltation
- Health
- Fruitfulness
- Victory
- God's favor

Who would not want to receive the blessings of God's abundant provision? Not only are they listed in the word of God for the nation of Israel, but also for us today.

2. Following after failures.

"He who cultivates his land will have plenty of bread, but he who follows worthless people and pursuits will have poverty enough" (Proverbs 28:19 - AMP).

There is an old leadership principle that says, *"If you're going to carry someone's briefcase, make sure it's someone who is going somewhere."* We must be careful to whom we attach ourselves, we may end up in a ditch. If we surround ourselves with people who are always doubting and critical, guess what we will become? We will become a person who is always doubting and criticizing.

If we hang out with people who have lousy attitudes, guess what we will have? We will have a lousy attitude! More than one parent has told a child, *"Tell me who you hang out with, and I will tell you who you are."* We are *who* we associate with. So if I want to become an Eagle Christian, I need to hang out with other Eagle Christians.

A wise person once said, *"Your friends will stretch your vision, or choke your dreams."*

People who are open for the chain of poverty are:

* Very critical of people who are doing something

in the Kingdom.

- Constantly looking for flaws in the lives of those who are prosperous.
- Always complaining about how others get the good things of life.
- Always blaming someone else for their failures.

3. Withholding more than you need.

> *"One person gives freely, yet gains even more; another withholds unduly, but comes to poverty"* (Proverbs 11:24 - NIV).

In the world system you are told that in order to get more you must invest more. To do that requires that you give up a sum of money in order to get a greater sum, right? There is a principle that every farmer knows called, "do not eat your best seed." It's exciting to walk into a blessing, but we must always be careful to invest back into the Kingdom to perpetuate the blessing.

Giving is a part of God's system. Everything He created was created to give. The greatest Bible verse ever given is one that most learn during childhood:

> *"For God so loved the world that he gave his one and only Son, that whoever*

believes in him shall not perish but have eternal life" (John 3:16 - NIV).

The emphasis is on "God gave!" God wanted sons, so what did He do? He gave His very best, His only Son in order to gain many sons for the Kingdom of God. You are a product of God's free gift. He did not withhold His best seed.

A person under the oppression of the spirit of poverty is always looking for a way to hold on to what they have. They live under the fear of "not having enough." When someone says, *"When I get some extra I'll give,"* is spoken out of doubt and fear, not faith. God does not reward doubt, only faith. Faith breaks the cycle of fear, and eliminates the excuses for withholding.

Malachi Chapter 1 illustrates how God feels about getting the leftovers from our lives. God chastised the people for giving Him their moulded bread, blind goats, lame sheep, and sick cows. In the process of giving God the scraps they:

• Doubted God's love (verse 2).
• Despised God's name (verse 6).
• Defiled God's altar (verses 7 – 10).

God demands our best because He gave His best for us! When faith goes to work, something happens in the spirit world that may not be seen right away. But it's happening, just like putting seed into the ground, or a woman during pregnancy.

> *"I will prevent pests from devouring your crops, and the vines in your fields will not drop their fruit before it is ripe," says the Lord Almighty"* (Malachi 3:11 - NIV).

4. Get rich quick motivation.

> *"A faithful person will be richly blessed, but one eager to get rich will not go unpunished"* (Proverbs 28:20 - NIV).

God is not opposed to you walking in riches. But if that is your motivation, it will lead to poverty. People who have a "get rich quick" motivation will not maintain what they have for very long. There are some who say we should never "give" in order to "get." That's not the problem. The problem comes when we view God as someone who can be bribed. God is not some kind of slot machine in the sky that if you put in enough money you will get a big payoff one day.

I know you have read or heard horror stories of people who won the lottery, who ended up broke at best and dead at worst. Many articles have been written about what people do with sudden riches. Many times they just couldn't handle it because there wasn't a foundation of integrity and honesty before God. The very thing they thought they wanted ended up destroying them.

Whether it's trying to hit the lottery or some other new scheme that comes along, it will never replace sound Biblical principles!

> *"Be careful that you do not forget the LORD your God, failing to observe his commands, his laws and his decrees that I am giving you this day. Otherwise, when you eat and are satisfied, when you build fine houses and settle down, and when your herds and flocks grow large and your silver and gold increase and all you have is multiplied, then your heart will become proud and you will forget the LORD your God, who brought you out of Egypt, out of the land of slavery. He led you through the vast and dreadful wilderness, that thirsty and waterless land, with its venomous snakes and scorpions. He*

brought you water out of hard rock. He gave you manna to eat in the wilderness, something your ancestors had never known, to humble and test you so that in the end it might go well with you. You may say to yourself, "My power and the strength of my hands have produced this wealth for me." But remember the LORD your God, for it is he who gives you the ability to produce wealth, and so confirms his covenant, which he swore to your ancestors, as it is today" (Deuteronomy 8:11-18 - NIV).

God makes it very clear in this passage that His desire is to establish His covenant. He wants His people to be able to use every financial resource to spread the Gospel. When God's desires become man's desires, He has already broken a strong link in the chain of poverty.

5. Neglecting the Material Needs of the Work of God

This is what the Lord Almighty says: "These people say, 'The time has not yet come to rebuild the Lord's house.'

Then the word of the Lord came through

the prophet Haggai: 'Is it a time for you yourselves to be living in your panelled houses, while this house remains a ruin?'

Now this is what the LORD *Almighty says: 'Give careful thought to your ways. You have planted much, but harvested little. You eat, but never have enough. You drink, but never have your fill. You put on clothes, but are not warm. You earn wages, only to put them in a purse with holes in it.'*

This is what the LORD *Almighty says: 'Give careful thought to your ways. Go up into the mountains and bring down timber and build my house, so that I may take pleasure in it and be honored,' says the Lord. 'You expected much, but see, it turned out to be little. What you brought home, I blew away. Why?' declares the Lord Almighty. 'Because of my house, which remains a ruin, while each of you is busy with your own house'"* (Haggai 1:2-9).

During the time of the Old Testament the temple or the tabernacle was referred to as the house of God.

Today, it's not the buildings that are the house of God, but the people. The buildings are the "home" of the Church, not the Church itself.

Verse 8 tells them to go to the mountaintop to get the necessary materials, come down, and build. Today, we have received an abundance of revelation on the mountaintop and we have a responsibility to take it to others. How? We give our time, talent and treasure to make sure that what we have been blessed with is shared around the world. Each time we plant the seed of the Gospel; we are sowing seeds that build up the "house" of God, i.e. the people of God.

It is very possible for a Church to be equipped with all of the nice things of the modern world, and still have the spirit of poverty ruling it. Some spend more time and money on buying the biggest and the best, while neglecting the very mandate of Jesus who told us to *"Go into all the world and spread the Good News!"*

6. Disunity.

> *"There was a man all alone; he had neither son nor brother.*

There was no end to his toil, yet his eyes were not content with his wealth. 'For whom am I toiling,' he asked, 'and why am I depriving myself of enjoyment?' This too is meaningless—a miserable business!

Two are better than one, because they have a good return for their labor: If either of them falls down, one can help the other up.

But pity anyone who falls and has no one to help them up. Also, if two lie down together, they will keep warm. But how can one keep warm alone? Though one may be overpowered, two can defend themselves. A cord of three strands is not quickly broken" (Ecclesiastes 4:8-12 - NIV).

Being a loner leads to poverty. Men have not learned the potential power that could be released from unity and corporate anointing. We can do greater things through uniting our time and resources than doing it alone.

"Behold, how good and how pleasant it is for brethren to dwell together in unity! It

is like the precious oil upon the head, running down on the beard, The beard of Aaron, Running down on the edge of his garments. It is like the dew of Hermon, Descending upon the mountains of Zion; For there the Lord commanded the blessing — Life forevermore" (Psalm 133 - NKJV).

Unity is not simply an intellectual exercise. We can believe the same things, recite the same creeds, belong to the same denomination, but that does not mean we have unity.

I came across this article by a well-known author. His name is Larry Crabb. Let me share it with you:

"Which is worse? A Church program to build community that doesn't get off the ground or one person sitting every Sunday in the back of the Church who remains unknown? A Sunday school class that once drew hundreds but has now dwindled to thirty or a Sunday school teacher whose sense of failure is never explored by a caring friend? A family torn apart by the Father's drinking, his wife's frustration, and their

third grader's learning disabilities or a self-hating dad, a terrified mom, and a lonely little boy, three human beings whose beauty and value no one ever discovers?

A national campaign that fails to gain steam for the pro-life movement or a single woman on her way home from an abortion clinic in the backseat of a taxi, a woman whose soul no one ever touches?"

We may notice the unknown pew sitter, we wonder how the teacher of the now small class feels, we worry over each member of the torn-up family, and we feel for the guilt and pain of a woman who has ended her baby's life. But we do what's easier. We design programs, we brainstorm ways to build attendance, and in our outrage over divorce statistics and abortion numbers we fight for family values.

These are all good things, but we don't TALK to the pew sitter; we don't ASK the teacher how he's feeling; we don't INVITE the dad to play golf, the woman to lunch, or the little boy to play with our children; we don't let the aborting woman know we CARE about her soul.

That response to hurting people, I would label disunity. Disunity is not just fighting over personal preferences. It's not just leaving the Church because someone hurt your feelings. It's not just gossip that tears down other members of the body. It's leaving needs unmet. It's failing to love people the way God would have us love. Unity is lived out in caring concern for others."
- *Soul Talk* by Larry Crabb

7. Slothfulness.

Sloth is one of the most dangerous links in the chain of poverty. Sloth means: a dis-inclination to action or labor. You can be "busy" and still be slothful! This is a demonic spirit and must be dealt with.

"That ye be not slothful, but followers of them who through faith and patience inherit the promises" (Hebrews 6:12).

"I went by the field of the slothful, and by the vineyard of the man void of understanding; And, lo, it was all grown over with thorns, and nettles had covered the face thereof, and the stone wall thereof was broken down. Then I saw, and considered it well: I looked upon it, and received instruction. Yet a little sleep, a little slumber, a little folding of the hands to sleep: So shall thy poverty come as one that travelleth; and thy want as an armed man" (Proverbs 24:30-34).

"Slothfulness casteth into a deep sleep; and an idle soul shall suffer hunger" (Proverbs 19:15).

Slothfulness occurs when we do not remain in "motion" with our God-given vision. There are too many "Dead Sea Christians." They are taking in and never giving out! We mustn't get hooked on yesterday's glory and success and let slothfulness rob us of tomorrow's dreams.

LIVING IN THE FLOW OF SUPERNATURAL ABUNDANCE

God is Able

> *"And God is able to make all grace abound toward you, that you, always having all sufficiency in all things, may have an abundance for every good work"* (2 Corinthians 9:8 - NKJV).

How is it possible to stay in the flow of perpetual blessing and abundance? One thing I know is we do not serve a stingy God who only gives just enough to sustain us. What does the Bible say about Him? He is the God of abundance!

1. The fullness of God.

Ephesians 3:19 (NKJV) declares, *"...that you may be filled with all the fullness of God."* The word "fullness" is taken from the root word "pleroma," which means: a full measure, plenitude that which has been totally completed in every way. This word is often used to describe a ship with a full cargo and crew. Fullness emphasizes completion. Our God wants nothing missing in our lives. His desire is for us to be full in every way. When Jesus died on the cross He said, *"It is finished!"*

It doesn't matter where you are in life. Where you are going does not depend on where you are right now. You are on a journey, and all that is important is to know God's will for your life is fullness and completion in every aspect.

Jesus said in John 15:11 (NKJV), *"These things I have spoken to you, that my joy may remain in you, and that your joy may be full."* It is the will of God that His joy should remain in us and He wants our joy to be full. He is a giver of good gifts, and a rewarder of those who diligently seek Him. Every good and perfect gift comes from our Father of light.

In the Old Testament, God told Abraham, *"Do not be afraid, Abram, I am your shield, your exceedingly great reward."* It would be easy to think that Abraham was such a great man of faith, and you are not, so therefore you do not qualify. No! You are a child of God and the seed of Abraham. God is as committed to you as he was to Abraham.

Who is Abraham's Seed?

> *"So in Christ Jesus you are all children of God through faith, for all of you who were baptized into Christ have clothed yourselves with Christ. There is neither Jew nor Gentile, neither slave nor free, nor is there male and female, for you are all one in Christ Jesus. If you belong to Christ, then you are Abraham's seed, and heirs according to the promise"* (Galatians 3:26-29 - NIV).

The apostle Paul makes it very clear if you are a believer in Jesus Christ, you are an inheritor of this awesome promise made to Abraham.

God actually swears this oath by Himself, the highest form of an oath possible in heaven or Earth. The writer of the book of Hebrews explains how this oath was given:

> *"When God made his promise to Abraham, since there was no one greater*

for him to swear by, he swore by himself saying, "I will surely bless you and give you many descendants." And so after waiting patiently, Abraham received what was promised.

People swear by someone greater than themselves, and the oath confirms what is said and puts an end to all argument. Because God wanted to make the unchanging nature of his purpose very clear to the heirs of what was promised, he confirmed it with an oath. God did this so that, by two unchangeable things in which it is impossible for God to lie, we who have fled to take hold of the hope set before us may be greatly encouraged" (Hebrews 6:13-18 - NIV).

Another aspect of this marvelous promise is that no discrimination is allowed. Galatians 3:28 (NIV) says, *"There is neither Jew nor Greek, there is neither slave nor free, there is neither male nor female; for you are all one in Christ Jesus."*

Being the seed of Abraham transcends the issue of race and class, and precludes gender discrimination (neither male nor female). It does not matter your race, economic or social background, or gender. This promise to Abraham belongs to all believing Christians! The promise will bring about unparalleled fruitfulness and blessings in the lives of all believers. It guarantees triumph over all enemies, and opens up the potential for blessing all nations (literally people groups) around the world. Those are not my promises; it is backed by the highest oath in the universe.

Staying in the flow of perpetual abundance is not a theory to be discussed, but a reality to be believed and lived. David, the man after God's own heart, said in Psalm 23:5 (NKJV), *"My cup runs over."* David was talking about the overflow. If you keep filling a full vessel it will overflow. Are you willing to be a vessel of overflow? Just containing what God wants you to have is not abundance. When abundance comes, it is without measure. When we get in line with the word of God, we will see the overflow.

Abundance is not given to us so that we can store it up and use it just for ourselves. I call it the Luke 6:38 (NKJV) principle, *"Give and it shall be given to you: good measure, pressed down, shaken together and running over will be put into your bosom. For with the same measure that you use, it will be measured back to you."*

Notice the words here ... *good measure, pressed down, shaken together and running over.* These are words to describe how God wants to give back to us. When we open our hands to God, He unlocks the windows of heaven to pour out abundance so great we will be amazed and astounded at the awesomeness of God. The apostle Paul put it this way in Ephesians 3:20 (NKJV), *"Now to Him who is able to do exceedingly abundantly above all that we ask or think, according to the power that works in us."*

It is important that we have a proper perspective regarding God's blessings upon our lives. He does not promise to pour out abundance and overflowing bounty because we deserve it or because we think we're better than others. His flow of abundance is based on our obedience to His word.

> *"Bring the whole tithe into the storehouse, that there may be food in my house. Test me in this," says the* LORD *Almighty, "and see if I will not throw open the floodgates of heaven and pour out so much blessing that there will not be room enough to store it"* (Malachi 3:10 - NIV).

The opening of the windows of heaven does not happen by accident or by chance. It requires obedience to God's command.

How to Stay in the Flow

We find in the New Testament Paul's admonition to the Church at Corinth. In his first letter to the Church he talked about taking up a "relief offering" for the poor Christians in Judea. This was not the first time he assisted in this way. Paul lived by the "forgotten beatitude" of Jesus who said, *"It is more blessed to give than to receive"* (Acts 20:35 - NIV).

Paul revealed the truth behind our giving and taught us how to stay in the perpetual flow of abundance. As we read his second letter, we discover the Corinthians were not doing their part. Like many people, they had made promises, but they failed to keep them. In fact, an entire year had gone by and nothing happened. I'm sure there were many reasons given as to why they did not follow through with their commitment. Paul knew it would be difficult to get them to participate, so he lifted his teaching to the highest spiritual level possible. He taught them that giving was an act of grace in spite of circumstances (see 2 Corinthians 8:1–2). He wanted them to give, not out of obligation, but as a demonstration of the working of the grace of God in their hearts.

Paul refers to the Macedonian Churches in Chapter 8 as an example of grace giving in spite of *"A great trial of affliction"* (vs. 2). The Macedonian Churches needed no prompting or reminding, as did the Church at Corinth. They not only suffered affliction, but also were in deep poverty. They had hit "rock–bottom destitution." They did not allow their circumstances to hinder them from giving joyfully and liberally.

There is a great difference between promise and performance. A year before these Corinthians had boasted they would share in the collection, but did not keep their promise. It is one thing to be willing, but the "doing" must follow. Having a sincere desire alone does not translate into action. You may have a sincere desire to walk in abundance, but unless you're willing to obey the word, it will not happen.

It seems strange that we as Christians have to be encouraged to give, when our Father has given so much to us. He demonstrated that He is the prime mover in giving. One verse of scripture that we all learned from our childhood and often forget sums it up this way. *"For God so loved the world that he gave his one and only Son, that whoever believes in him shall not perish but have eternal life"* (John 3:16).

Paul was trying to show the Corinthians how God enriched them in a wonderful way, and yet they were reluctant to share with others. As Paul explained the "grace giving" approach to get involved in the special offering for the suffering Church, he gave them five encouragements related to grace giving. In doing so he wanted them to understand that to get in the flow of perpetual abundance, it had to start with them. A tight-fisted, stingy people, will never get involved in the flow of abundance even though they know the abundant blessings they have received from God.

1. When you give, it encourages others.

> *"There is no need for me to write to you about this service to the Lord's people. For I know your eagerness to help, and I have been boasting about it to the Macedonians, telling them that since last year you in Achaia were ready to give; and your enthusiasm has stirred most of them to action. But I am sending the brothers in order that our boasting about you in this matter should not prove hollow, but that you may be ready, as I said you would be. For if any Macedonians come with me and find you unprepared, we—not to say anything about you—would be ashamed of having been so confident. So I thought it*

necessary to urge the brothers to visit you in advance and finish the arrangements for the generous gift you had promised. Then it will be ready as a generous gift, not as one grudgingly given" (2 Corinthians 9:1-5 - NIV).

The apostle Paul was not urging them to compete with others concerning their sacrifice and service. Paul sent Titus and the other brothers to Corinth to stir them up to share in the offering. Far more important than the money was the spiritual benefit that would come to them as they shared in response to God's grace in their lives.

Our greatest encouragement for giving is not because we feel pressure, but because it blesses our Lord. Our obedience can provoke others to give. Our motive is not to boast, but to encourage.

2. Your giving will bless you.

"But this I say: He who sows sparingly will also reap sparingly, and he who sows bountifully will also reap bountifully. So let each one give as he purposes in his heart, not grudgingly or of necessity; for God loves a cheerful giver. And God is

able to make all grace abound toward you, that you, always having all sufficiency in all things, may have an abundance for every good work. As it is written: He has dispersed abroad, He has given to the poor, His righteousness endures forever.

Now may He who supplies seed to the sower, and bread for food, supply and multiply the seed you have sown and increase the fruits of your righteousness, while you are enriched in everything for all liberality, which causes thanksgiving through us to God" (2 Corinthians 9:6-11 - NKJV).

Remember the Lord's promise, *"Give, and it shall be given unto you,"* still holds true (see Luke 6:38). The "good measure" He gives back to us is in direct relation to what has been given. It may not always be money or material goods, but it is always worth far more than we gave.

Giving is not something we do, but something we are. For the Christian who understands "grace giving," it is a way of life, not sporadic or capricious. Those who do not understand how the principal of abundance works, can never understand a statement like Proverbs 11:24, *"One person gives freely, yet gains even more; another withholds unduly, but comes to poverty."*

Paul outlines for us these principles to remember:

- *The Principle of Increase*: we reap in measure as we sow (vs. 6). We see this principle operating in everyday life. Every farmer knows that the more seed he plants in the ground, the better chance for a greater harvest. When you take a large investment of money to the bank, it will certainly collect more interest. The more we invest in the Gospel of Jesus Christ, the more "fruit" will abound to our account (Philippians 4:10–20).

- *The Principal of Intent*: we reap as we sow with the right motives (vs. 7). To the farmer who plants his seed, motive makes no difference. If he sows good seed in good ground with good weather, he will reap a harvest. The Christian is different. Motive in giving or any other activity is vitally important. Paul is clear; giving must come from the heart to please God, not men.

May it never be said of us that we are "sad givers" who give grudgingly, or "mad givers" because we must. We should be "glad givers" who cheerfully share what we have because of the many blessings that God has given us. *"He that has a bountiful eye shall be blessed"* (Proverbs 22:9).

- *The Principle of Immediacy:* we reap even while we are sowing (vs. 8–11). While it is true the farmer has to wait for his harvest, the believer who practices grace giving begins to reap immediate abundance. Yes, some harvest takes longer than others to be sure there are long-range benefits, but there are also immediate blessings to enjoy.

Notice the word "abundance." God is able to make it happen for us. When? Always, in all things! In essence, it is God's will that we never lack at any point in time, and there is no deficiency, but *all sufficiency.*

The perpetual flow of *supernatural abundance* means: all grace always; all sufficiency for every good work. The word "sufficiency" means: adequate resources within (see Philippians 4:11).

We may go through a valley of lack for a season, but we don't stop in the valley. How else will we know our God is the abundant supplier of more than enough if we never experience a "need?"

Need is an interesting word. The definition of need is: a lack of something requisite, desirable, or useful, a condition requiring supply or relief. We don't like to talk about having "needs." It almost sounds like that we don't have faith for the abundant supply. God has some unusual ways of getting our attention. He never seems to get our attention through success, but in our distresses.

> *"Hear me when I call, O God of my righteousness: thou hast enlarged me when I was in distress; have mercy upon me, and hear my prayer"* (Psalm 4:1).

I'm sure you've noticed that every miracle in the Bible started with a need. Without needs you will never know He is the God of miracles. You may need a miracle as big as parting the Red Sea; but, *"Stand still and see the salvation of the Lord."* Or it may be as small as paying your utility bill. Size is not the issue, it's a matter of recognizing that, *"And my God shall supply all your need according to His riches in glory by Christ Jesus"* (Philippians 4:19 - NKJV).

The Perpetual Flow of Supernatural Abundance has a Purpose

It is not for our selfish motives God wants to give us abundance so we can hoard all things for ourselves. It pleases the heart of God to see us enjoying his abundant provision, but that is not the ultimate purpose. The apostle Paul makes it clear we may have, *"abundance for every good work."* The purpose of abundance is for what He calls us to do we will have complete and total sufficiency for everything within our sphere or calling. So many times when we feel prompted by the Holy Spirit to respond, we have had to say "No" because we don't have the resources for the task.

The early Church didn't respond with a "No." They simply said, *"Lord, You give us direction and we will go."* Their attitude was much different than today's Church that depends so much on money. Of course we must be wise in handling money. But so many Churches are tied down by budgets. I wonder what it would be like if we made decisions not by how much we have, but simply on what God is calling us to do, and leave the resources up to Him. I am convinced that God would bankrupt heaven to supply the overflow of abundance to any ministry that would totally surrender and sell out to do His will on planet

Earth!

There is so much more to abundance than just giving and receiving.

> *"One specific good work for which God provides abundance is the primary "good work": that we may provide Him a dwelling place. The purpose of God from creation onward has been to dwell with man. We often talk as though the ultimate for us is to get to heaven. In reading the Bible, however, I find that the ultimate is to get heaven to Earth. In the closing chapters of the Bible, we do not find Earth going up to heaven; we find heaven coming down to Earth. The ultimate thrust of God's purpose from creation onward is to dwell with man. Consider two historic examples in the Bible where God asked His people Israel, to provide for him a dwelling place. The first dwelling place was the Tabernacle of Moses. The second was at the Temple of Solomon. In each case God provided His people with abundance in advance, that out of their abundance they might return to Him all that would be needed*

to provide Him a dwelling place suitable to His glory."
-*The Promise of Provision*: by Derek Prince:

First the Natural then the Spiritual

In the days of Israel we saw the building of the tabernacle of Moses and David, as well as the Temple of Solomon. But in our day it's not the physical building God is concerned about. The purpose of God in our day is to *dwell* with man.

What we see in the natural in the Old Testament is revealed to a higher spiritual level in the New Testament.

> *"Do you not know that you are the temple of God and that the Spirit of God dwells in you? If anyone defiles the temple of God, God will destroy him. For the temple of God is holy, which temple you are"* (1 Corinthians 3:16–17 - NKJV).

Where is God's dwelling place today? Peter says in 1 Peter 2:5, *"You also, as living stones, are being built up a spiritual house, a holy priesthood."*

In other words, we are a dwelling place for the Holy

Spirit of God. Just as God dwelt with His people, Israel, in the Old Testament temple, so He dwells with His people in a New Temple. The Spirit of God dwells in each of us. We are the temple of God. We are a dwelling place for the Holy Spirit. We are people through whom God manifests His glory.

The Bible teaches that we are to be conformed to the image of Jesus Christ. That is God's purpose for us. God is changing us daily into the image of His Son. Now this image is an inward image, not an outward one. God gives us His moral attributes: love, peace, purity, justice, fairness, and so much more. They are imparted to us as we allow Holy Spirit to live in and through our lives. This is God's plan for us. It is His plan for His Church.

While man builds beautiful structures that cost millions of dollars, this does not impress God. What God wants is infinitely more precious than gold and silver. His desire is a dwelling place in and among His people. The Old Testament structures, though beautiful and costly, were temporary. Only remnants are left today.

Make no mistake about it; God will be no less particular and lavish about His ultimate, eternal dwelling place, which is you and me.

"For thus says the LORD of hosts: 'Once more (it is a little while) I will shake heaven and Earth, the sea and dry land; and I will shake all nations, and they shall come to the Desire of All Nations, and I will fill this temple with glory,' says the LORD of hosts. 'The silver is Mine, and the gold is Mine,' says the LORD of hosts. 'The glory of this latter temple shall be greater than the former,' says the LORD of hosts. 'And in this place I will give peace,' says the LORD of hosts" (Haggai 2:6-9 - NKJV).

Haggai was not talking about a temple that was destroyed, but pointing to a time in the future when the Lord says, *"I will fill this temple with glory."* What Temple is He speaking of? Not some new structure erected in Israel, as some believe. He is talking about "living stones," not dead concrete. In these last days God is pouring out the perpetual flow of abundance to bring His people into a completed body.

Isaiah looked through time and saw the same thing:

"Arise, shine, for your light has come, and the glory of the LORD rises upon you. See, darkness covers the Earth and thick darkness is over the peoples, but the LORD

rises upon you and his glory appears over you. Nations will come to your light, and kings to the brightness of your dawn.

Lift up your eyes and look about you: All assemble and come to you; your sons come from afar, and your daughters are carried on the hip. Then you will look and be radiant, your heart will throb and swell with joy; the wealth on the seas will be brought to you, to you the riches of the nations will come" (Isaiah 60:1-5 - NIV).

The question is: what is the real purpose of the abundant flow? If God says, *"The riches of the nations will come."* what will be the purpose of all this wealth? Will it be to build bigger and better? Will it be to build a bigger name for ourselves?

The wealth of the nations is connected to God's glory filling the Earth, and building a dwelling place suited for Him. Not a building, but millions and millions of people who make up living stones, people who will have the resources and abundance available to reach many more millions, who have yet to receive Jesus Christ.

"When you focus on being a blessing, God makes sure that you are always blessed in abundance." ~ Joel Osteen

"The test of our progress is not whether we add more to the abundance of those who have much it is whether we provide enough for those who have little." ~ Franklin D. Roosevelt

"Abundance is not something we acquire. It is something we tune into." ~ Wayne Dyer

"Abundance is a process of letting go; that which is empty can receive." ~ Bryant H. McGill

"Instead, I have an abundance mentality: When people are genuinely happy at the successes of others, the pie gets larger." ~ Stephen Covey

"Expect your every need to be met. Expect the answer to every problem, expect abundance on every level." ~ Eileen Caddy

"You pray in your distress and in your need; would that you might also pray in the fullness of your joy and in your days of abundance." ~ Khalil Gibran

"You have to think anyway, so why not think big?" ~ Donald Trump

"Plant seeds of happiness, hope, success, and love; it will all come back to you in abundance. This is the law of nature." ~ Steve Maraboli

"When you are grateful, fear disappears and abundance appears." ~ Anthony Robbins

"People with a scarcity mentality tend to see everything in terms of win-lose. There is only so much; and if someone else has it, that means there will be less for me. The more principle-centered we become, the more we develop an abundance mentality, the more we are genuinely happy for the successes, well-being, achievements, recognition, and good fortune of other people. We believe their success adds to…rather than detracts from…our lives." ~ Stephen R. Covey

"Start with big dreams and make life worth living." ~ Stephen Richards

"Life in abundance comes only through great love." ~ Elbert Hubbard

"Whatever we are waiting for – peace of mind, contentment, grace, the inner awareness of simple abundance – it will surely come to us, but only when we are ready to receive it with an open and grateful heart." ~ Sarah Ban Breathnach

"The world is full of abundance and opportunity, but far too many people come to the fountain of life with a sieve instead of a tank car… a teaspoon instead of a steam shovel. They expect little and as a result they get little." ~ Ben Sweetland

"Abundance is about being rich, with or without money." ~ Suze Orman

"I keep the telephone of my mind open to peace, harmony, health, love and abundance. Then whenever doubt, anxiety, or fear try to call me, they keep getting a busy signal and soon they'll forget my number." ~ Edith Armstrong

For more information on our upcoming conferences, international ministry trips, or to purchase books, eBooks, mp3s, CDs or DVDs from our web store, please visit our website globalmissionawareness.com.

MORE FROM LEIF HETLAND:

In this metaphorical and biblical journey, Leif Hetland shares a story based on a vision God gave him several years ago. It is a story that can transform our minds and reveal God's desire to bring His Supernatural Abundance to every part of our lives.

Also available in Ebook

All that the Father has is ours! All creation is groaning for the sons and daughters to be revealed. It is time for us to come into the fullness of who we were created to be so all creation will come back to the Father's house.

Available in Paperback and Ebook

A worldview that will transform your life...This beautifully written memoir-essay explores the realities of Papa God's love for you, your destiny as His beloved child and heir, and the transformation of your vision of yourself, others, and world events that this revelation of your place in the divine family brings

Available in Hardback and Paperback

Through this manual, listen to the hearts of Leif Hetland and Paul Yadao as they lead you into: The heart of soaking, Being still to hear His voice, The rhythm of heaven, and Creating a culture of soaking.

Available in Paperback (8.5 x 11 or 6 x9) and Ebook

The Garden of Eden was a place of perfect peace, security, beauty, creativity and love. It was in this place where God the Father and Adam dreamed together. Discover God's heart for you and your dream life by creating an atmosphere to dream with Papa God.

Available in DVD and CD

One of Leif's most popular messages! All of us operate from one of three chairs: Commitment, Compromise or Conflict. Learn where you are and how to stay in Chair #1.

Available in DVD, MP3 and CD

GlobalMissionAwareness.com
PO Box 3049
Peachtree City, GA 30269
770.487.4800

Made in the USA
Charleston, SC
25 July 2014